Just For The HEALTH Of It

Simple Diabetes Recipes
Everyone Will Enjoy

BARBARA MOULTON

iUniverse, Inc.
Bloomington

Just For The Health Of It
Simple Diabetes Recipes Everyone Will Enjoy

iUniverse books may be ordered through booksellers or by contacting:

iUniverse
1663 Liberty Drive
Bloomington, IN 47403
www.iuniverse.com
1-800-Authors (1-800-288-4677)

ISBN: 978-1-4620-0331-0 (sc)
ISBN: 978-1-4620-0332-7 (ebook)

Printed in the United States of America

iUniverse rev. date: 5/13/2011

Dedication

To my dear husband, mother, father, family, and friends. Your encouragement and support has made all the difference. Thank you to Robin Spencer Photography for the amazing photos and cover design. Thank you to those recipe tasters for your feedback and support. To those who suffer, may the burden of diabetes be lightened. B.M.

Contents

Appetizers and Beverages

*A wonderful start to any meal or just
something yummy to munch on!*

Tip: These guys are known for being small but calories ar
carbohydrates can add up fast. Be sure to limit the amount an
most importantly include them in your meal plan.

Cheese Breadsticks

Prep: 5 min   Cook: 10 min

1 tube (11 ounces) refrigerated breadsticks
1 teaspoon light ranch dressing
2 tablespoons grated Parmesan cheese

Preheat oven to 375 degrees.

Unroll breadsticks, separate, and place on a baking sheet. In a small bowl, mix dressing and cheese with a spoon. Using fingers, lightly spread cheese mixture over breadsticks. Bake 10–12 minutes until light golden brown. Makes 6 servings of 2 breadsticks each.

Nutrition information: calories: 120, calories from fat 29, total fat 3 grams, saturated fat <1 gram, cholesterol 1 gram, sodium 321 milligrams, carbohydrates 18 grams, fiber <1 gram, sugar 1 gram, protein 3 grams, Exchanges: 1 starch, 1/2 fat.

Pizza Pillows

Prep: 10 min Cook: 15 min

1 can (13 ounces) refrigerator French bread
5 mozzarella cheese sticks
½ cup pizza sauce
1 tablespoon parmesan cheese, shredded

Preheat oven to 350 degrees. Unroll bread dough onto a cutting board. Use a pizza cutter to cut into 24 equal pieces. Cut cheese sticks into 5 pieces each. Place ½ teaspoon of pizza sauce and 1 piece of cheese in the center of each piece of dough. Fold dough over and pinch sides to secure. Place on prepared cookie sheet. Spray pillows with pan spray and sprinkle shredded cheese over top of pillows. Bake for 15 minutes. Makes 24 servings.

Nutrition information: calories 62, calories from fat 14, saturated fat 1 gram, cholesterol 7 milligrams, sodium 182 milligrams, carbohydrate 7 grams, fiber <1 gram, sugar <1 gram, protein 4 grams. Exchanges: starch ½.

Dip in pizza sauce or light ranch dressing.

Deluxe Chicken Nachos

Prep: 15 min Bake: 7 min

2 4-ounce boneless skinless chicken breasts, diced
1 clove garlic, minced
1/3 cup water
1 teaspoon garlic powder
1 teaspoon onion powder
1 teaspoon cumin
1/2 teaspoon chili powder
About 60 tortilla chips
2 Roma tomatoes, diced
3/4 cup grated Mexican cheese blend
2 green onions, chopped
1 can (2.25 ounces) chopped black olives, drained

Preheat oven to 350 degrees.

In a frying pan, sauté chicken and garlic with water and seasonings until chicken juices run clear. Arrange chips on a baking sheet. Spoon cooked chicken mixture over chips. Layer tomatoes, cheese, onions, and olives over chips. Bake for 5–7 minutes until cheese melts. Makes 8 servings.

Nutrition information: calories 266, calories from fat 80, total fat 8 grams, saturated fat 3 grams, cholesterol 90 milligrams, protein 36 grams, carbohydrate 10 grams, fiber 1 gram, sugar 1 gram, sodium 264 milligrams. Exchanges: Starch 1 very lean meat 4 ½, vegetable 1/2, fat 1.

Bacon Ranch Dip

Prep: 2 min. plus refrigeration time

1 container (16 ounces) fat free sour cream
1 envelope (1.12 ounce) ranch dressing seasoning mix
1 tablespoon soft bacon bits

In a small bowl, combine all ingredients until mixed well. Refrigerate for 3–4 hours. Serve chilled. Makes 32 (1/2 tablespoon) servings.

Nutrition information: calories 14, calories from fat <1, total fat <1 gram, Sat fat <1 gram, cholesterol 10 milligrams, sodium 130 milligrams, protein 2 grams, carbohydrate 2 grams, fiber <1 gram, sugar <1 gram. Exchanges: 0.

Family Crab Dip

Prep: 2 min plus refrigeration time

1 package (8 ounces) low fat cream cheese, softened
1 container (16 ounces) fat free sour cream
1 envelope (1.12 ounce) ranch dressing mix
16 ounces imitation crabmeat

Use an electric hand mixer to combine cream cheese, sour cream, and dressing mix until well blended. Stir crabmeat pieces into mixture. Chill for one hour or until ready to serve. Makes 32 (2 tablespoon) servings.

Nutrition information: calories 57, calories from fat 17, total fat 2 grams, saturated fat 1 gram, cholesterol 15 milligrams, sodium 276 milligrams, carbohydrate 4 grams, fiber 0, sugar 0, protein 4 grams. Exchanges: very lean meat 1/2.

Spinach and Chive Dip

Prep: 6 min plus refrigeration time

10 ounces chopped frozen spinach, thawed
1 can (8 ounces) sliced water chestnuts, drained
1 container (16 ounces) fat free sour cream
4 tablespoons chives, chopped
1 packet (.46 ounce) vegetable dip mix
1/2 cup skim milk

Drain any excess water from spinach. Dice water chestnuts into fine pieces. Combine spinach, water chestnuts, and remaining ingredients until well blended. Chill for one hour or until ready to serve. Makes 32 (2 tablespoon) servings.

Nutrition information: calories 19, calories from fat 2, protein 1 gram, carbohydrate 2 grams, sugar 1 gram, total fat <1 gram saturated fat <1 gram, cholesterol 10 milligrams, fiber <1 gram, sodium 42 milligrams. Exchanges: 0.

Baked Layered Bean Dip

Prep: 10 min Cook: 10 min

2 cans (15.4 ounces each) organic fat free refried beans
1 teaspoon garlic powder
1 teaspoon onion powder
1 teaspoon cumin
1/2 teaspoon chili powder
1 container (16 ounces) fat free sour cream
1 can (2.25 ounces) sliced black olives, drained
2 small tomatoes, diced
2 green onions, thinly sliced
1 cup grated Mexican cheese blend

Preheat oven to 350 degrees.

In a large bowl, mix beans and seasonings. Spray baking dish with nonstick cooking spray. Spread bean mixture over the bottom of 7 x 11 baking dish. Evenly spread sour cream over beans. Top with olives, tomatoes, and onions. Sprinkle cheese over all. Bake for 10–15 minutes until cheese is melted. Makes 24 (1/4 cup) servings.

Nutrition information: calories 72, calories from fat 21, total fat 2 grams, saturated fat <1 grams, cholesterol 17 milligrams, sodium 243 milligrams, carbohydrate 9 grams, fiber 2 grams, sugar 2 grams, protein 4 grams. Exchanges: starch 1/2.

Note: Organic refried beans are used in this recipe because of the lower sodium content.

Veggie Bites

Prep: 12 min   Cook: 10 min

1 tube (8 ounces) reduced fat refrigerated crescent rolls
1/2 package (8 ounces) fat free cream cheese
3/4 cup fat free sour cream
1/4 cup low fat ranch salad dressing
1 tablespoon soft bacon bits
1 small cucumber, sliced
1 cup fresh chopped broccoli
1 cup cherry tomatoes
3 tablespoons sliced black olives

Preheat oven to 375 degrees.

Unroll crescent rolls on the bottom of 9 x 13-inch pan prepared with cooking spray. Press triangles together to form a rectangle crust. Bake for 10 minutes or until golden brown. Allow crust to cool completely.

Beat cream cheese, sour cream, dressing, and bacon bits until smooth. Spread cream cheese mixture over baked crust. Arrange vegetables evenly over top. Cut into 20 squares using a pizza cutter. Refrigerate until ready to serve. Makes 20 servings.

Nutrition information: calories 71, calories from fat 24, total fat 3 grams, saturated fat <1 gram, cholesterol 7 grams, sodium 255 milligrams, carbohydrate 9 grams, fiber <1 gram, sugar 2 grams, protein 2 grams. Exchanges: starch 1/2, fat 1/2.

Corn Bread Bites

Prep: 5 min   Cook: time varies

2 boxes (8.5 ounces each) corn bread muffin mix
2 egg whites
1/2 cup frozen corn, thawed
2/3 cup unsweetened applesauce

Preheat oven to 400 degrees.

In a medium bowl, mix together all ingredients until moistened. Drop into miniature muffin cups sprayed with nonstick cooking spray. Bake for 7–9 minutes until golden brown. Makes 35 servings.

Nutrition information: calories 48, calories from fat 13, total fat 1 gram, saturated fat <1 gram, cholesterol 9 milligrams, sodium 112 milligrams, carbohydrate 8 grams, fiber <1 gram, sugar 2 grams, protein 1 gram. Exchanges: starch 1/2.

Yummy Punch

Prep: 5 min

1 1/2 cups orange juice
1/2 cup pineapple juice
1 cup fresh or frozen strawberries
2 cups ice
2 liters diet lemon-lime soda

Place juice and fruit in a blender. Top with ice and blend until well mixed and ice is in small pieces. In a large punch bowl, stir fruit mixture together with soda. Serve immediately. Makes 8 (1 1/2 cup) servings.

Nutrition information: calories 28, calories from fat 0, total fat 0 grams, saturated fat 0 grams, cholesterol 0 grams, sodium 44 milligrams, carbohydrate 7 grams, fiber <1 gram, sugar 6 grams, protein <1 gram. Exchanges: fruit 1/2.

Strawberry Delight Smoothie

Prep: 5 min

2 cups thawed frozen strawberries, with juice
1 cup skim milk
2 containers (6 ounces each) sugar free strawberry yogurt
2 cups ice cubes
1 cup water

Place strawberries, milk, yogurt, and ice, and water in a blender. Blend until smooth. Makes 5 (1 cup) servings.

Nutrition information: calories 74, calories from fat 2, total fat <1 gram, saturated fat <1 gram, cholesterol 3 milligram, sodium 59 milligrams, carbohydrate 13 grams, fiber 1 gram, sugar 9 grams, protein 4 gram. Exchanges: fat free milk 1.

Stuffed Mushrooms

Prep: 20 min Bake: 6-8

25 medium white mushrooms
8 ounces fat free cream cheese, softened
¼ teaspoon Worcestershire sauce
¼ teaspoon onion powder
1 tablespoon soft bacon bits
1 tablespoon parmesan cheese, shredded

Preheat oven to 350. Wash and remove stems from mushrooms. Set aside. Combine cream cheese, Worcestershire sauce, onion powder, bacon bits, and cheese. Spoon cream cheese mixture into mushrooms tops. Bake on a cookie sheet for 6-8 minutes. Serve immediately. Makes 25 servings.

Nutrition information: calories 20, calories from fat 3, total fat <1 gram, saturated fat<1 gram, cholesterol 2 milligrams, sodium 64 milligrams, carbohydrate <1 gram, fiber<1 gram, sugar <1 gram, protein 2 grams. Exchanges: 0.

Soup, soup, soup

A welcomed delight on a cold day or night!

Tip: Soup add-ons such as crackers, cheese, and chips can quickly add on more carbohydrates and fat.

Italian Ham and Bean Soup

Pre: 6 min   Cook: 10 min

1 bag (16 ounces) frozen Italian vegetables
1 can (15 ounces) low salt garbanzo beans, drained
1 can (15.25 ounces) low salt kidney beans, drained
1 can (14.5 ounces) low salt diced tomatoes, with liquid
6 ounces Canadian bacon, diced
2 cans (11.5 ounces each) low sodium chicken broth
1 cup water
1/2 teaspoon garlic powder
1/2 teaspoon onion powder

Combine all ingredients in a 4- to 6-quart stock pot. Slightly mash tomatoes. Stir to combine. Bring soup to boiling. Reduce heat and simmer 7–9 minutes. Makes 11 (1 cup) servings.

Nutrition information: calories 139, calories from fat 17, total fat 2 grams, saturated fat <1 gram, cholesterol 8 milligrams, sodium 181 milligrams, carbohydrate 20 grams, fiber 6 grams, sugar 3 grams, protein 10 grams. Exchanges: starch 1, lean meat 1, vegetable 1.

Hearty Tortellini Soup

Prep: 10 min Cook: 20 min

1/4 cup chopped onion
1 tablespoon olive oil
3 chicken breasts, diced
9 cups water, divided
1 bag (16 ounces) frozen California blend vegetables
7 to 8 low sodium chicken bouillon cubes
2 teaspoons Italian seasoning
1/4 teaspoon pepper
2 tablespoons white or wheat flour
5 cups frozen cheese tortellini

In a 5- to 7-quart stockpot, sauté onion in olive oil until tender. Add chicken pieces and 1 cup water. Cook until chicken is no longer pink in center. Add remaining water, vegetables, bouillon cubes, Italian seasoning, pepper, and flour. Wisk flour and seasonings until evenly mixed. Bring soup to a hard boil. Add tortellini. Let boil 3–4 minutes until heated through and all tortellini floats to the top. Makes 11 (1 cup) servings.

Nutrition information: calories 210, calories from fat 59, total fat 7 grams, saturated fat 1 gram, cholesterol 34 milligrams, sodium 258 milligrams, carbohydrate 20 grams, fiber 2 grams, sugar 3 grams, protein 17 grams. Exchanges: starch 1, very lean meat 2, fat 1/2, vegetable 1/2.

Note: Wheat flour tortellini can be substituted in this recipe.

Green Chili Chicken Soup

Prep: 5 min   Cook: 20 min

3 large chicken breasts
1/2 cup chopped onion
2 cloves garlic, minced
1 can (14 ounces) low sodium vegetable broth
4 cups low sodium chicken broth
1 can (16 ounces) green chili enchilada sauce
2 cups water

In a 4-quart saucepan, cook chicken breasts, onion, and garlic in broth for 20–25 minutes. Shred chicken as it cooks. Add chili enchilada sauce and water. Simmer for 7–9 minutes. Makes 10 (1 cup) servings.

Nutrition information: calories 89, calories from fat 25, total fat 2 grams, saturated fat <1 gram, cholesterol 25, sodium 244 milligrams, carbohydrate 3 grams, fiber <1 gram, sugar <1 gram, protein 12 grams, Exchanges: very lean meat 1/2.

Note: Soup may be garnished with tortilla chips, shredded cheese, or light sour cream.

Baked Chicken Potato Soup

Prep: 10 min Cook: 60 min

2 boneless, skinless chicken breasts, diced
3 red potatoes, diced
1 cup chicken broth
1/4 cup diced onion
2 cups frozen carrot coins
2 celery ribs, sliced
1/2 teaspoon basil
1 teaspoon garlic powder
1 teaspoon onion powder
1 teaspoon salt
1/2 teaspoon pepper
2 cups water

Preheat oven to 350 degrees.

Place chicken and potatoes in a 9 x 13-inch pan that has been prepared with nonstick cooking spray. Add remaining ingredients except water. Gently stir to combine. Drizzle water over mixture. Cover with aluminum foil and bake for 1 hour. Makes 8 servings (1 cup each)

Nutrition information: calories 63, calories from fat 6, total fat <1 gram, saturated fat <1 gram, cholesterol 20 milligrams, sodium 218 milligrams, carbohydrate 4 grams, fiber 1 gram, sugar 1 gram, protein 9 grams. Exchanges: very lean meat 1, vegetable 1/2.

Grandpa's Favorite Soup

Prep: 6 min   Cook: 20 min

3 skinless, boneless chicken breasts, cooked
3 cans (14.5 ounces each) low sodium chicken broth
2 cups cooked instant brown or white rice
1 1/2 cups low sodium tomato juice
1 can (4 ounces) chopped green chilies, drained
2 cups frozen corn
1 cup salsa

Shred chicken with a fork. Combine chicken with all ingredients in a 5- to 7-quart saucepan. Simmer for 20 minutes or until heated through. Makes 12 servings (1 cup each).

Nutrition information: calories 252, calories from fat 42, total fat 5 grams, saturated fat <1 gram, cholesterol 83 milligrams, sodium 257 milligrams, carbohydrate 16 grams, fiber 1 gram, sugar 4 grams, protein 37 grams. Exchanges: starch 1, very lean meat 4 1/2, vegetable 1.

Note: May garnish with crushed tortilla chips, shredded cheese, or light sour cream.

Chicken Chili

Prep: 10 min Cook: 10 min

1 pound chicken breasts
3 cups water, divided
1 jar (16 ounces) chunky salsa
2 cans (15.5 ounces each) low sodium dark red kidney beans,
    drained
1 can (14.5 ounces) stewed tomatoes, with liquid
1 cup frozen corn
2 teaspoons garlic powder
2 teaspoons cumin
2 teaspoons chili powder
1/4 teaspoon salt
1/8 teaspoon pepper

In a 4-quart stockpot, cook chicken over medium heat in 1/2 cup water. Break up into bite size pieces while cooking. Add salsa, beans, tomatoes, corn, remaining water, and spices. Stir to mix completely. Simmer for 10 minutes or until heated through. Makes 10(1 cup) servings.

Nutrition information: calories 157, calories from fat 6, total fat <1 gram, saturated fat <1 gram, cholesterol 8 milligrams, sodium 141 milligrams, carbohydrate 26 grams, fiber 9 grams, sugar 3 grams, protein 12 grams. Exchanges: starch 2, very lean meat 1.

Note: May garnish with tortilla chips or serve with corn bread bites (see appetizers).

Chunky Taco Soup

Prep: 6 min   Cook: 30 min

1 pound lean ground beef
1/2 cup chopped onion
2 cups frozen corn
2 cans (14.5 ounces each) stewed tomatoes, with liquid
2 cans (15.5 ounces each) low sodium red kidney beans, drained
1 teaspoon garlic powder
1 teaspoon cumin
1/2 teaspoon ground chili powder
1 can (8 ounces) low sodium tomato sauce
1 tablespoon brown sugar

Brown ground beef and onion together in a 4-quart stockpot. Drain any excess fat if needed. Stir in remaining ingredients. Simmer at least 30 minutes over medium heat. Makes 10(1 cup) servings.

Nutrition information: calories 281, calories from fat 70, total fat 7 grams, saturated fat 3 grams, cholesterol 36 milligrams, sodium 193 milligrams, carbohydrate 31 grams, fiber 10 grams, sugar 7 grams, protein 21 grams. Exchanges: starch 2, lean meat 2.

Note: Garnish with crushed tortilla chips, shredded cheese, or light sour cream.

Meatless Country Chili

Prep: 10 min   Cook: 15 min (stove top) 3-4 hours (slow cooker)

1 can (28 ounces) whole peeled tomatoes with liquid, chopped
1 can (15 ounces) reduced sodium, black beans, rinsed and
   drained
1 can (16 ounces) red kidney beans, rinsed and drained
1 can (16 ounces) chili beans in sauce, with liquid
1 can (15 ounces) whole kernel corn, with liquid
2 cans (8 ounces each) low sodium tomato sauce
1 medium onion, chopped
1 cup chopped green bell pepper
8 ounces fresh mushrooms, sliced
2 tablespoons Italian seasoning
2 tablespoons minced garlic
2 tablespoons chili powder
½ teaspoon garlic pepper

Combine all ingredients in a 5- to 6-quart slow cooker sprayed
with nonstick cooking spray. Cover and cook on high heat for 3–4
hours or on low heat for 6–8 hours. Makes 15 (1 cup) servings.

Nutrition information: calories 131, calories from fat 6, total fat
<1 gram, saturated fat <1 gram, cholesterol 0 milligrams, sodium
122 milligrams, carbohydrate 24 grams, fiber 7 grams, sugar 6
grams, protein 7 grams. Exchanges: starch 1 ½.

Quick Homemade Stew

Prep: 6 min   Cook: 10 min

1 pound stew meat, fat removed
3 cups water, divided
1 envelope beef gravy mix
1/2 teaspoon Italian seasoning
3 cups frozen diced potatoes, thawed
1 bag (16 ounces) frozen Italian mixed vegetables, thawed
1 can (10.5 ounces) reduced fat mushroom soup, condensed
1 1/2 cups skim milk
1/4 cup white or wheat flour

In a 5- to 7-quart stockpot, brown meat in one cup water, occasionally stirring. Add remaining water, seasonings, potatoes, and vegetables. Bring to a boil and simmer 7–9 minutes. Stir to blend.

In a separate bowl, combine milk and flour. Stir flour mixture into soup until blended and slightly thickened. Heat through and serve warm. Makes 10 (1 cup) servings.

Nutrition information: calories 196, calories from fat 80, total fat 9 grams, saturated fat 4 grams, cholesterol 33 milligrams, sodium 317 milligrams, carbohydrate 17 grams, fiber 2 grams, sugar 3 grams, protein 11 grams. Exchanges: starch 1, lean meat 1, vegetable 1, fat 1.

Hamburger Vegetable Soup

Prep: 6 min   Cook: 10 min

1 pound lean ground beef
1 jar (26 ounces) reduced sugar spaghetti sauce
4 cups low sodium beef broth
1 package (16 ounces) frozen California mix vegetables
8 ounces fresh mushrooms, sliced
1/4 cup diced onion
1 cup water

Brown ground beef in a 3- to 4-quart soup pan. Drain any excess fat if necessary. Add spaghetti sauce and broth; bring to a boil. Add frozen vegetables, mushrooms, and onion, and water. Return to boil and cook until vegetables are heated through and mushrooms are reduced. Makes 10 (1 cup) servings.

Nutrition information: calories 168, calories from fat 84, total fat 9 grams, saturated fat 3 grams, cholesterol 31 milligrams, sodium 431 milligrams, carbohydrate 8 grams, fiber 3 grams, sugar 5 grams, protein 13 grams. Exchanges: starch1/2, lean meat 1 1/2, vegetable 1, fat 1.

Note: Serve with homemade wheat rolls.

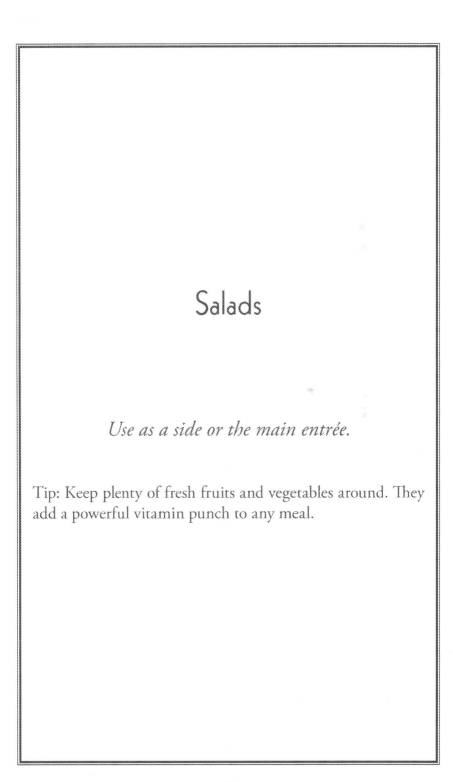

Salads

Use as a side or the main entrée.

Tip: Keep plenty of fresh fruits and vegetables around. They add a powerful vitamin punch to any meal.

Spinach Strawberry Salad

Prep: 7 min

1/2 cup poppy seed salad dressing
1/2 cup water
1 bag (6 ounces) mixed spinach salad
1 cup grated mozzarella cheese
1 1/2 cups sliced strawberries
4 ounces fresh mushrooms, sliced
2 tablespoons chopped pecans

Mix poppy seed dressing with water and refrigerate. Layer spinach, cheese, strawberries, mushrooms, and pecans in a serving bowl. Refrigerate until ready to use. Toss salad with dressing immediately before serving. Makes 9 (1 cup) servings.

Nutrition information: calories 91, calories from fat 70, total fat 8 grams, saturated fat 1 gram, cholesterol 1 milligram, sodium 208 milligrams, carbohydrate 2 grams, fiber <1 gram, sugar <1 gram, protein 2 grams. Exchanges: fat 1.

Cabbage Salad

Prep: 8 min

1 package (3 ounces) oriental flavored ramen noodles
2 boneless skinless chicken breasts, cooked and diced
1 bag (16 ounces) coleslaw cabbage and carrot salad
2 tablespoons sunflower seeds
2 tablespoons slivered almonds
2 green onions, sliced
1/4 cup canola oil
2 tablespoons vinegar
1 teaspoon sugar

Set aside ramen seasoning packet for later use. Break noodles into bite size pieces. In a large bowl, combine dry noodles, chicken, cabbage, sunflower seeds, almonds, and onions. In a separate bowl, mix canola oil, vinegar, sugar, and seasoning packet until well blended. Chill salad and dressing separately. Just before serving, pour dressing over cabbage and ramen mixture. Cover salad and toss until evenly coated. Eat immediately for best quality. Cover and store in the refrigerator. Makes 12 (1 cup) servings.

Nutrition information: calories 129, calories from fat 75, total fat 8 grams, saturated fat 1 gram, cholesterol 11 milligrams, sodium 178 milligrams, carbohydrate 7 grams, fiber 1 gram, sugar 1 gram, protein 5 grams. Exchanges: starch 1/2, very lean meat 1/2, fat 1.

Lisa's Summer Salad

Prep: 7 min

3/4 cup reduced fat blue cheese dressing
1 cup cold water, divided
2 boneless skinless chicken breasts
2 tablespoons chicken grill seasoning
1 bag (16 ounces) green salad mix
1 small avocado, peeled, cored, and sliced
1 cup cherry tomatoes
1/3 medium red onion, thinly sliced

Mix salad dressing with 3/4 cup cold water and chill. In a frying pan, cook chicken with seasoning and 1/4 cup water until no longer pink in center. Slice or break into small pieces. In a salad bowl, layer salad, cooled chicken, avocado, tomatoes, and onion. Chill salad until ready to serve. Serve with dressing on the side. Makes 10 (1 cup) servings.

Nutrition information: calories 261, calories from fat 98, fat 11 grams, saturated fat <1 gram, cholesterol 82 milligrams, sodium 284 milligrams, carbohydrate 5 grams, fiber 3 grams, sugar 3 grams, protein 35 grams. Exchanges: very lean meat 4 1/2, vegetable 1, fat 1.

Variation: Ranch dressing can be substituted for blue cheese.

Grandma's Salad

Prep: 5 min plus chill time

7 cups chopped broccoli florets
25 cherry tomatoes
1 can (6 ounces) medium pitted black olives, drained
1 cup fat free Italian dressing
2 tablespoons grated Parmesan cheese

Combine broccoli, tomatoes, and olives in a 2- to 3-quart bowl. Pour salad dressing over top. Cover and gently toss salad to allow dressing to cover as many vegetables as possible. Refrigerate covered salad for 6–24 hours. Gently toss periodically. Serve chilled with cheese sprinkled over the top. Makes 14 (3/4 cup) servings.

Nutrition information: calories 51, calories from fat 22, total fat 2 gram, saturated fat <1 gram, cholesterol <1 milligram, sodium 280 milligrams, carbohydrate 5 grams, fiber 1 gram, sugar 2 grams, protein 1 gram. Exchanges: vegetable 1 1/2.

Tomato Cucumber Salad

Prep: 7 min

1/2 medium red onion
1 can (6 ounces) black olives, drained
2 medium cucumbers
4 medium tomatoes

Dressing:
1/4 cup vinegar
2 tablespoons olive oil
1 tablespoon honey
1/2 teaspoon dried basil
1/4 teaspoon garlic powder
1/8 teaspoon dried oregano
1/2 teaspoon salt
Dash pepper

Slice red onion thinly and place in a 2-quart bowl. Slice cucumbers and cut slices into halves. Cut tomatoes into 1/2-inch chunks. Add cucumber, olives and tomato to onion. In a small bowl, mix together vinegar, oil, honey, and spices. Stir together dressing and vegetables and chill for 1 hour. Makes 8 (1 cup) servings.

Nutrition information: calories 87, calories from fat 53, total fat 6 grams, saturated fat <1 gram, cholesterol 0 milligrams, sodium 279 milligrams, carbohydrate 7 grams, fiber 1 gram, sugar 5 grams, protein 1 gram. Exchanges: carbohydrate ½, vegetables 1, fat 1.

Broccoli Supreme Salad

Prep: 5 min

3/4 cup light mayonnaise
1 teaspoon vinegar
1 teaspoon salad seasoning
1/2 cup raisins
1 cup grapes, sliced in half
2 tablespoons pecans, chopped
1 large head (6 cups) broccoli, cut into bite size pieces
3 tablespoons bacon pieces

In a small bowl, whisk first three ingredients until well blended. In a large bowl, combine remaining ingredients. Slightly toss together to make uniform. Add mayonnaise mixture to broccoli mixture and stir until salad is uniformly coated. Refrigerate until ready to serve. Cover and store in the refrigerator. Makes 14 (3/4 cup) servings.

Nutrition information: calories 95, calories from fat 40, total fat 4 grams, saturated fat 1 grams, cholesterol 7 milligrams, sodium 441 milligrams, carbohydrate 11 grams, fiber 1 gram, sugar 8 grams, protein 3 grams. Exchanges: fruit 1/2, vegetable 1 1/2, fat 1/2.

Bean and Salsa Salad

Prep: 7 min   Cook: 10 min

2 boneless skinless chicken breasts
1/4 cup water
1 envelope reduced sodium taco seasoning
1 can (15 ounces) organic pinto beans, drained
1 cup frozen whole kernel corn, thawed
3/4 cup salsa
1 bag (16 ounces) green salad mix
3/4 cup grated cheddar cheese

Cut chicken into bite size pieces and cook in water and taco seasoning until no longer pink and juices run clear. Combine chicken, beans, corn, and salsa. Cover and simmer for 10 minutes. Serve over lettuce mixture and top with cheese. Makes 8 (1/2 cup) servings.

Nutrition information: calories 149, calories from fat 46, total fat 5 grams, saturated fat 2 grams, cholesterol 27 milligrams, sodium 242 milligrams, carbohydrate 14 grams, fiber 4 grams, sugar 2 grams, protein 13 grams. Exchanges: starch 1, very lean meat 1, vegetable 1, fat ½.

Note: This salad can be served cold by chilling chicken mixture after cooking.

Creamy Pasta Salad

Prep: 10 min   Cook: according to package directions

1 package (13.25 ounces) regular or whole grain elbow noodles
1/2 cup light mayonnaise
1/4 cup light ranch dressing
1 teaspoon salt
1 teaspoon mustard
1 tablespoon soft bacon bits
1 teaspoon lemon juice
1 cup peas, frozen, thawed
1/2 cup diced cheddar cheese
1 cup sliced black olives
1 small tomato, diced
1 medium cucumber, quartered and sliced

Cook pasta according to package directions. Drain in a colander and rinse with cold water until cool. Mix mayonnaise, dressing, salt, mustard, bacon bits, and lemon juice until blended. In a large bowl, combine noodles, peas, cheese, olives, tomato, and cucumber. Stir in dressing until blended. Chill. Makes 14 (1 cup) servings.

Nutrition information: calories 161, calories from fat 53, total fat 6 grams, saturated fat 1 gram, cholesterol 7 milligrams, sodium 303 milligrams, carbohydrate 20 grams, fiber 3 grams, sugar 2 grams, protein 6 grams. Exchanges: starch 1, fat 1.

Chilled Tortellini Salad

Prep: 5 min   Cook: according to package directions

4 cups frozen cheese tortellini
8 ounces pre-sliced fresh mushrooms
2 tablespoons water
3/4 cup fat free Italian salad dressing
2 tablespoons diced red onion
1 medium tomato, diced
2 tablespoons grated Parmesan cheese

Cook tortellini according to package directions. Cool in a colander under cold water and set aside. In a frying pan, sauté mushrooms in 2 tablespoons water. Transfer tortellini to a serving bowl. Gently toss tortellini with salad dressing, mushrooms, red onion, and tomato. Chill for at least 1 hour. Garnish with cheese before serving. Makes 10 (1 cup) servings.

Nutrition information: calories 125, calories from fat 25, total fat 2 grams, saturated fat 1 gram, cholesterol 9 milligrams, sodium 345 milligrams, carbohydrate 19 grams, fiber 2 grams, sugar 2 grams, protein 6 grams. Exchanges: starch 1.

Note: Whole wheat tortellini may be substituted.

Creamy Fruit Salad

Prep: 6 min

1 box (1 ounce) sugar free vanilla pudding mix
1 container (6 ounces) light vanilla yogurt
1/2 cup skim milk
1 container (8 ounces) frozen sugar free whipped topping,
    thawed
2 cups sliced strawberries
1 1/2 cups grapes, halved
1 large banana, peeled and sliced
1 can (20 ounces) pineapple tidbits, drained

Combine pudding mix, yogurt, and milk until well blended. Fold in whipped topping. Add all fruit into pudding mixture and stir until mixed through. Refrigerate until ready to serve. Makes 8 (1 cup) servings.

Nutrition information: calories 161, calories from fat 34, total fat 4 grams, saturated fat 3 grams, cholesterol <1 gram, sodium 76 milligrams, carbohydrate 29 grams, fiber 1 gram, sugar 21 grams, protein 1 gram. Exchanges: fruit 1, fat free milk 1.

Savory Vegetables

*A powerful antioxidant fighting
snack that travels well.*

Tip: If you are trying to lose weight, add more non starchy vegetables to your meals and snacks. Go easy with butter, dips, and sauces.

Old Fashioned Green Beans

Prep: 2 min   Cook: 10 min

1 bag (16 ounces) frozen cut green beans
3 tablespoons diced onion
2 tablespoons soft reduced fat bacon pieces (optional)

Place frozen green beans in a medium saucepan. Cover with water. Add onion and bacon pieces. Simmer until onion is tender. Makes 7 (1/2 cup) servings.

Nutrition information: calories 20, calories from fat 3, total fat <1 gram, saturated fat <1 gram, cholesterol 2 milligrams, sodium 52 milligrams, carbohydrate 3 grams, fiber 1 gram, sugar 1 gram, protein 1 gram. Exchanges: vegetable 1.

Buttery Dill Baby Carrots

Prep: 2 min   Cook: 10 min

1 pound baby carrots
2 tablespoons butter
1/2 tablespoon dried dill
1 teaspoon lemon juice
1/8 teaspoon lemon pepper

In a 2-quart saucepan, cover carrots with water. Boil carrots for 15 minutes or until tender. Drain water from carrots. Stir butter, dill, lemon juice, salt, and pepper into carrots. Serve immediately. Makes 4 (1 cup) servings.

Nutritional information: calories 70, calories from fat 30, total fat 3 grams, saturated fat <1 gram, cholesterol 7 milligrams, sodium 70 milligrams, carbohydrate 10 grams, fiber 2 grams, sugar 5 grams, protein 1 gram. Exchanges: carbohydrate ½, vegetable 2, fat 1/2.

Hot Mushroom and Zucchini Blend

Prep: 5min   Cook: 8 min

2 small zucchini, sliced
1/2 cup water
8 ounces pre-sliced fresh mushrooms
3 green onions, sliced
2 tablespoons fat free Italian dressing
1/2 teaspoon salt
1/2 teaspoon pepper
2 tablespoons grated Parmesan cheese

Sauté zucchini slices in water until slightly tender. Add mushrooms and green onion. Add Italian dressing and continue cooking for one minute. Remove from heat. Sprinkle with salt, pepper, and Parmesan cheese. Serve warm. Makes 6 (1/2 cup) servings.

Nutrition information: calories 24, calories from fat 6, fat <1 gram, saturated fat <1 gram, cholesterol 2 milligrams, sodium 194 milligrams, carbohydrate 3 grams, fiber 1 gram, sugar 1 gram, protein 1 gram. Exchanges: 0.

Seasoned Potatoes

Prep: 10 min Cook: 40 min

2 pounds small red potatoes
3 tablespoons olive oil
1 teaspoon garlic powder
2 tablespoons reduced sodium chicken grill seasoning

Preheat oven to 400 degrees.

Cut potatoes into large chunks. Place potatoes in a gallon-size re-closeable bag. Drizzle olive oil and seasonings over potatoes in bag. Close bag and shake until all potatoes are covered with seasoning. Arrange potatoes on a large baking sheet. Bake for 40 minutes until potatoes are lightly browned and tender. Makes 5 (1 cup) servings.

Nutrition information: calories 133, calories from fat 70, total fat 8 grams, saturated fat <1 gram, cholesterol 0 milligrams, sodium 345 milligrams, carbohydrate 13 grams, fiber 5 grams, sugar 1 gram, protein 3 grams. Exchanges: starch 1, fat 1.

Savory Balsamic Garden Asparagus

Prep: 7 min   Bake: 12-14min

1 pound fresh asparagus
Vegetable oil cooking spray
2 tablespoons butter
1 tablespoon low sodium soy sauce
1 tablespoon balsamic vinegar
1 teaspoon packed brown sugar

Preheat oven to 400 degrees.

Break the very bottom ends off the asparagus. Place asparagus on a baking sheet. Spray asparagus with cooking spray. Bake for 12–14 minutes until soft tender. In a small saucepan, melt butter over medium heat. Once melted, stir in soy sauce, vinegar, and brown sugar. Remove from heat, and drizzle sauce over baked asparagus. Makes 4 servings.

Nutrition information: Calories 59, calories from fat 25, total fat 3 grams, saturated fat <1 gram, cholesterol 7 milligrams, sodium 182 milligrams, carbohydrate 7 grams, fiber 2 grams, sugar 4 grams, protein 3 grams. Exchanges: vegetable 1.

Vegetable Stir-Fry

Prep: 10 min Cook: 15 min

2 slices onion quartered and rings separated
1 small zucchini, sliced
1 bag (16 ounces) frozen stir-fry vegetables
8 ounces pre-sliced fresh mushrooms
1/3 cup stir-fry sauce
1/2 cup chopped roasted cashew nuts

Cut onion into 1-inch pieces and cook in a frying pan prepared with nonstick cooking spray until tender-crisp. Add remaining vegetables and cook until heated through. Add sauce and continue cooking for additional 2 minutes. Top with cashews before serving Makes 5 (1 cup) servings.

Nutrition information: calories 144, calories from fat 54, total fat 6 grams, saturated fat 1 gram, cholesterol 0 grams, sodium 528 milligrams, carbohydrate 18 grams, fiber 3 grams, sugar 7 grams, protein 5 grams. Exchanges: starch ½, vegetable 1 1/2, fat 1.

Note: Serve with brown or white rice if desired.

Flavorful Cashew Broccoli

Prep: 5 min   Cook: 7 min

1 1/2 pounds fresh broccoli, cut into pieces
1/3 cup butter
1 tablespoon brown sugar
2 tablespoons low sodium soy sauce
1 tablespoon Worcestershire sauce
2 teaspoons balsamic vinegar
1/4 teaspoon pepper
½ teaspoon onion powder
2 cloves garlic, minced
1/3 cup chopped salted cashews

In a large soup pan, place broccoli in 1 inch water and bring to a boil, cooking for 7 minutes until tender. While broccoli cooks, melt butter in a small sauce pan. Stir in brown sugar, sauces, vinegar, pepper, onion powder, and garlic. Bring sauce to a boil, and then remove from heat. Drain broccoli, and spoon into a serving dish. Sprinkle cashews over top of broccoli. Pour sauce over top and serve immediately. Makes 10 (1/2 cup) servings.

Nutrition information: calories 80, calories from fat 43, total fat 5 grams, saturated fat 2 grams, cholesterol 8 milligrams, sodium 187 milligrams, carbohydrate 7 grams, fiber <1 grams, sugar 3 grams, protein 3 grams. Exchanges: vegetable 1.

Veggie Subs

Prep: 8 min   Cook: 3-5 min

6 wheat hoagie buns
1/4 cup light ranch dressing, divided
1 red bell pepper, sliced thin
1 can (2.25 ounces) sliced black olives, drained
3 ½-inch onion slices, separated
1 8-ounce package pre-sliced fresh mushrooms
1 1/2 cups grated part skim mozzarella cheese
2 tablespoons grated Parmesan cheese
2 small tomatoes, sliced

Preheat broiler.

Cut hoagies in half lengthwise. Spread salad dressing evenly over one side of each bun. Arrange bell pepper, olives, onions, and mushrooms on both halves. Top with cheeses and broil for 3–5 minutes or until cheese is bubbly. Remove from oven and place tomato slices over half of sandwich. Put sandwich together and eat immediately or wrap firmly in foil until ready to eat. Cut in half at an angle while still in foil. Makes 6 servings.

Nutrition information: calories 232, calories from fat 88, total fat 10 grams, saturated fat 3 grams, cholesterol 13 milligrams, sodium 484 milligrams, carbohydrate 26 grams, fiber 4 grams, sugar 6 grams, protein 13 grams. Exchanges: starch 2, very lean meat 1, vegetable 1, fat 1.

Beef

A little goes a long way.

Tip: Choose cuts of meat with less marbling and remove all visible fat before cooking. Cuts with "round" or "loin" in the name are a healthy choice.

Seasoned Beef Kabobs

Prep: 12 min Cook: 10 min

1 pound boneless sirloin steak
1 small red onion
1 can (20 ounces) pineapple chunks, drained
8 ounces whole water chestnuts, drained
8 ounces whole fresh mushrooms
1/2 cup water
1/2 cup teriyaki sauce

Cut beef and onion into 1-inch chunks. Thread all ingredients except water and sauce in an alternating pattern on bamboo skewers. Combine water and teriyaki sauce and brush kabobs. Grill or broil for 10 minutes or until beef is done and vegetables are tender-crisp. Turn every few minutes through cooking time and brush with sauce. Makes 5 servings.

Note: bamboo skewers need to be soaked in water before using so they don't char or catch on fire.

Nutrition information: calories 351, calories from fat 98, total fat 11 grams, saturated fat 4 grams, cholesterol 80, sodium 427 milligrams, protein 30 grams, carbohydrate 32 grams, fiber 4 grams, sugar 21 grams. Exchanges: starch 1, very lean meat 4, vegetables 1, fruit 1.

Rubbed Steak and Salsa

Prep: 10 min Cook: 10 min

1 1/2 pounds sirloin steak
1 1/2 tablespoons chili powder
1/2 teaspoon dried oregano
1 teaspoon garlic powder
1/2 cup chunky salsa
1/3 cup enchilada sauce
1 small tomato, diced
2 tablespoons diced red onion
1/2 cup black beans, rinsed and drained
2 tablespoons chopped fresh cilantro

Preheat broiler.

Rinse and pat steaks dry. Combine chili powder, oregano, and garlic powder, and then rub seasoning mixture on both sides of steaks. Set aside. In a small bowl, combine remaining ingredients and then refrigerate. On a baking sheet, broil steaks 4–6 minutes. Turn over and cook an additional 1–3 minutes. Serve salsa with steak. Makes 6 servings.

Nutritional information: calories 264, calories from fat 135, total fat 15 grams, saturated fat 5 grams, cholesterol 71, sodium 321 milligrams, carbohydrate 6 grams, fiber 1 gram, sugar 2 grams, protein 26 grams. Exchanges: starch 1/2 lean meat 3, fat 1.

Steak and Rice Dinner

Prep: 5 min   Cook: according to package directions

1 package (7.2 ounces) herb and butter rice mix
1 pound sirloin steak, cut into 1-inch pieces
1/4 cup diced onion
1 8-ounce package pre-sliced fresh mushrooms
1 teaspoon olive oil

Prepare rice according to package directions. In a large frying pan, sauté steak, onions, and mushrooms in olive oil until vegetables are tender and meat reaches desired doneness. Stir meat mixture into cooked rice mixture. Makes 6 (1 cup) servings.

Nutritional information: calories 273, calories from fat 108, total fat 11 grams, saturated fat 3 grams, cholesterol 67 milligrams, sodium 338 milligrams, carbohydrate 15 grams, fiber <1 gram, sugar <1 gram, protein 25 grams. Exchanges: starch 1, lean meat 3 1/2.

Garlic Rubbed Roast

Prep: 10 min Bake: 1-2 hours

2 pounds roast
1 teaspoon Italian seasoning
1 teaspoon garlic powder
1 slice red onion, separated into rings
3 medium potatoes, diced
12 ounces petite baby carrots
1 8-ounce package pre-sliced fresh mushrooms
1/3 cup water

Preheat oven to 350 degrees.

Remove all visible fat from meat. Mix together Italian seasoning and garlic powder and then rub onto roast. Center roast in a 9 x 13-inch pan. Arrange onion, potatoes, carrots, and mushrooms around roast. Pour water over all. Cover and bake 1 hour. Makes 6 servings.

Nutrition information: calories 323, calories from fat 64, total fat 7 grams, saturated fat 2 grams, cholesterol 80 milligrams, sodium 125 milligrams, carbohydrate 26 grams, fiber 3 grams, sugar 5 grams, protein 38 grams. Exchanges: starch 2, lean meat 4, vegetable 1.

Note: Gravy can be made using the drippings from the pan after cooking.

Inside-Out Enchiladas

Prep: 15 min Cook: 25 min

1 pound lean ground beef
1 can (10 ounces) red enchilada sauce
1 can 2.25 ounces sliced black olives
1 can 4 ounce green chilies, drained
1 1/2 cups mozzarella cheese
12 6-inch flour or corn tortillas
1 1/2 cups grated taco blend cheese

Preheat oven to 350 degrees.

In a 4-quart sauce pan, cook beef until no longer pink and juices run clear. Drain if necessary. Add sauce; simmer over low heat for 15 minutes. While simmering, heat tortillas, one at a time, in a medium frying pan sprayed with nonstick cooking spray. Combine olives, chilies, and cheese until blended. Arrange 2 tablespoons cheese mixture down the center of each heated tortilla. Roll up tightly and place in an 11 x 7-inch pan prepared with nonstick cooking spray. Snugly place tortillas in pan. Top with 1 1/2 cups of meat mixture over enchiladas. Cover and bake for 5–7 minutes or until cheese is melted. Serve with remaining meat mixture divided over each individual enchilada. Makes 12 servings.

Nutrition information: calories 225, calories from fat 97, total fat 10 grams, saturated fat 3 grams, cholesterol 40 milligrams, sodium 549 milligrams, carbohydrate 15 grams, fiber 9 grams, sugar 1 grams, protein 17 grams. Exchanges: starch 1, medium fat meat 2.

Note: Corn tortillas will need to be partially fried with cooking spray before preparation to prevent breakage.

Grandma's Favorite Lasagna

Prep: 10 min Cook: 60 min

1 jar (26 ounces) reduced sugar spaghetti sauce, plus 1 cup water
1 teaspoon Italian seasoning
1 pound ground beef, browned and drained
1/4 cup egg substitute
1 container (16 ounces) low fat cottage cheese
12 oven ready white or wheat lasagna noodles
4 ounces grated mozzarella cheese

Preheat oven to 350 degrees.

Spray bottom and sides of a 9 x 13-inch pan with nonstick cooking spray. Stir spaghetti sauce and Italian seasoning into cooked hamburger. Add water and stir. In a separate bowl, mix egg substitute with cottage cheese. Place a layer of uncooked noodles in pan, breaking to fit if necessary. Layer half meat sauce, half cottage cheese, and half mozzarella cheese over noodles. Repeat layers, starting with noodles and ending with mozzarella cheese. Cover and cook for 1 hour. Makes 12 servings.

Note: Regular cook noodles may be used but must be cooked before assembling lasagna.

Nutrition information: calories 242, calories from fat 83, total fat 9 grams, saturated fat 5 grams, cholesterol 31 milligrams, sodium 331 milligrams, carbohydrate 17 grams, fiber 3 grams, sugar 4 grams, protein 21 grams. Exchanges: starch 1, lean meat 3.

Chunky Vegetable Marinara Pasta

Prep: 10 min Cook: 12-15 min

1 package (14.5 ounces) regular or multi-grain elbow noodles
1 pound lean ground beef
1 small zucchini, sliced
8 fresh mushrooms, sliced
1/2 medium green bell pepper, diced
1/4 cup chopped onion
1 1/2 teaspoons Italian seasoning
2 cans (8 ounces each) reduced sodium tomato sauce
1 jar (26 ounces) no sugar added spaghetti sauce

Prepare noodles according to package directions. In a 4-quart stockpot, brown meat, draining if needed. Add vegetables to cooking meat and sauté until vegetables are tender. Stir in Italian seasoning. Stir in tomato and spaghetti sauces. Cook over medium heat until hot. Combine vegetable sauce with hot cooked noodles. Serve immediately. Makes 12 (1 cup) servings.

Nutritional information: calories 258, calories from fat 74, total fat 8 grams, saturated fat 3 grams, cholesterol 48 milligrams, sodium 238 milligrams, carbohydrate 28 grams, fiber 5 grams, sugar 5 grams, protein 18 grams. Exchanges: starch 2, lean meat 2, vegetable 1.

Western Style BBQ Meatloaf

Prep: 7 min   Cook: 45-55 min

1/4 cup egg substitute
1/4 cup dry oatmeal or bread crumbs
1 pound lean ground beef
1 teaspoon Italian seasoning
1/3 cup barbecue sauce, divided

Preheat oven to 350 degrees.

Mix together egg substitute, oatmeal, beef, Italian seasoning, and 1/2 of the barbecue sauce. Shape into a 9 x 5 inch bread pan. Pour remaining barbecue sauce over top and bake, uncovered, for 45–55 minutes. Makes 6 servings.

Nutrition information: calories 212, calories from fat 121, total fat 13 grams, saturated fat 5 grams, cholesterol 52 milligrams, sodium 252 milligrams, carbohydrate 6 grams, fiber <1 gram, sugar 3 grams, protein 15 grams. Exchanges: starch 1/2, lean meat 2, fat 1.

Ramen Noodle Stir-Fry

Prep: 6 min   Cook: 12 min

1 pound sirloin, cut into thin strips
2 cups water, divided
1 package (3 ounces) oriental flavored ramen noodles
1 package (16 ounces) fresh or frozen stir-fry vegetables
1 8-ounce package pre-sliced fresh sliced mushrooms
1/3 cup stir-fry sauce

Cook noodles according to package directions. Drain, set aside, and keep warm. In a large frying pan cook beef stirring occasionally for 5 minutes or until it reaches desired doneness. Add vegetables and mushrooms. Cover and cook 5 minutes or until vegetables are tender-crisp. In a small bowl stir together seasoning packet, stir-fry sauce, and 1 cup water until blended. Add sauce mixture and noodles. Stir occasionally and continue to cook until heated through. Add remaining water if needed. Makes 6 (1 cup) servings.

Nutrition information: calories 278, calories from fat 103, total fat 11 grams, saturated fat 4 grams, cholesterol 67 milligrams, sodium 662 milligrams, carbohydrate 16 grams, fiber 2 grams, sugar 3 grams, protein 25 grams. Exchanges: starch 1, very lean meat 3, vegetable 1, fat 1.

Note: This item may not be appropriate for a low sodium diet.

Salisbury Patties

Prep: 6 min   Cook: 20 min

2 pounds lean ground beef
1/2 cup dry bread crumbs
2 egg whites
1/3 cup chopped onion
1 teaspoon garlic pepper
1 8-ounce package pre-sliced fresh mushrooms
1 can (14 ounces) low sodium beef broth
1 teaspoon cornstarch
1 cup water, divided
1 can (10.5 ounces) reduced fat cream of mushroom soup,
   condensed

In a bowl, combine beef, bread crumbs, egg whites, onion, and garlic pepper. Form meat mixture into 10 patties. Cook in a medium to large frying pan until done. Remove from pan and keep warm. In same frying pan, combine mushrooms and broth. Simmer until mushrooms are tender. In a separate bowl, combine cornstarch and 1/4 cup water and stir into broth mixture. Continue to simmer until thickened. Stir in soup until smooth. Use remaining water to thin gravy to desired consistency. Serve warmed patties topped with mushroom gravy. Makes 10 (1 patty) servings.

Nutrition information: calories 281, calories from fat 146, fat 15 grams, saturated fat 6 grams, cholesterol 74 milligrams, sodium 382 milligrams, carbohydrate 7 grams, fiber <1 gram, sugar 1 gram, protein 25 grams. Exchanges: lean meat 3, fat1.

Taco Pot Pie

Prep: 10 min Cook: 20-25 min

1 pound ground beef
1/3 cup chopped onion
1 teaspoon garlic powder
1 teaspoon onion powder
1 teaspoon cumin
1/2 teaspoon chili powder
1 can (15.5 ounces) reduced sodium kidney beans, rinsed and
    drained
1 can (10 ounces) diced tomatoes and green chilies, drained
3/4 cup grated cheddar cheese
1 tube (8 ounces) refrigerated reduced fat crescent rolls

Preheat oven to 375 degrees. Prepare a 9 x 13-inch baking dish
with nonstick cooking spray.

Cook ground beef and onion until meat is no longer pink. Drain if
necessary. Add seasonings, beans, and tomatoes. Mix until blended.
Pour into baking dish. Sprinkle cheese over meat mixture. Unroll
crescent rolls and press perforated seals together. Place on top
of meat mixture, covering the top as much as possible. Bake for
20–25 minutes or until golden. Makes 8 (1 cup) servings.

Nutrition information: calories 313, calories from fat 123, total fat
11 grams, saturated fat 4 grams, cholesterol 48 milligrams, sodium
395 milligrams, carbohydrate 27 grams, fiber 7 grams, protein 20
grams. Exchanges: starch 2, lean meat 2, fat 1.

Seasoned Shredded Beef Sandwiches

Prep: 4 min   Cook: 6-8 hours

2 pounds chuck roast
1/2 envelope dry Italian salad dressing mix
1 tablespoon minced garlic
1 8-ounce package mushrooms, sliced
1/2 red onion, chopped
8 whole wheat hamburger buns

Place meat in a 3 1/2- to 4 1/2-quart slow cooker. Sprinkle dressing mix, garlic, mushrooms, and onion over the top. Cover and cook on low heat 7–9 hours. An hour before serving, remove any excess fat and shred meat with two forks. Cover and allow meat to simmer an additional 30-60 minutes on low heat. Divide meat mixture evenly over 8 warm hamburger buns. Serve immediately.

Nutritional information: calories 292, calories from fat 109, total fat 12 grams, saturated fat 4 grams, cholesterol 46 milligrams, sodium 566 milligrams, carbohydrate 30 grams, fiber 2 grams, sugar 3 grams, protein 16 grams. Exchanges: starch 2, lean meat 2, fat 1.

Finger-Lickin' Sloppy Burgers

Prep: 5 min   Cook: 10-15 min

1 1/2 pounds lean hamburger
2 tablespoons diced onion
1/2 medium green bell pepper, diced
1 clove garlic, minced
1/3 cup barbecue sauce
2 tablespoons ketchup
8 whole wheat hamburger buns

In a large frying pan, brown hamburger until no longer pink. Drain if necessary. Add onion, bell pepper, and garlic. Continue cooking until vegetables are tender-crisp. Stir in barbecue sauce and ketchup. Cook until heated through. Serve hot over warm hamburger buns. Makes 8 servings.

Nutrition information: calories 304, calories from fat 114, fat 12 grams, saturated fat 4 grams, cholesterol 53 milligrams, sodium 391 milligrams, carbohydrate 30 grams, fiber 1 gram, sugars 5 grams, protein 19 grams. Exchanges: starch 2, lean meat 2, fat 1.

Cowgirl Casserole

Prep: 7 min   Cook: 30 min

1 pound lean ground beef
1 can (15 ounce) chili
1 can (15 ounce kidney beans, rinsed and drained
1 can (14.5 ounce) Italian tomatoes
1 ½ cups frozen corn, thawed
½ cup fat free sour cream
5 cups tortilla chips, slightly crushed
1 cup cheese, shredded

Preheat oven to 400 degrees. In a 4-quart pot, brown hamburger until no longer pink. Drain if necessary. Add chili, beans, tomatoes, corn, and sour cream. Stir together. Prepare a 9 x 13 inch pan with non stick spray. Place tortilla chips in bottom of pan. Spoon meat mixture evenly over chips until covered. Top with cheese. Cover and bake for 30 minutes. Makes 12 servings.

Nutrition information: Calories 320, calories from fat 109, total fat 12 grams, saturated fat 6 grams, cholesterol 34 milligrams, sodium 526 milligrams, carbohydrate 38 grams, fiber 7 grams, sugar 2 grams, protein 16 grams. Exchanges starch 1 ½, lean meat 1 ½, fat 1, other carbohydrate 1.

Serve with a fresh garden salad.

Beef Fajitas

Prep: 40 min Cook: 15 min

1 1/2 pounds sirloin steak
2 tablespoons canola oil
1 tablespoon Worcestershire sauce
1 tablespoon lemon juice
1 teaspoon white vinegar
1/2 teaspoon cumin
1 large green bell pepper
1 medium red onion
1 envelope (1.12 ounces) fajita seasoning
2 small red tomatoes, diced
10 white flour or wheat tortillas

Cut beef into thin strips. Combine oil, Worcestershire sauce, lemon juice, vinegar, and cumin to form a marinade. Marinate beef strips in mixture for at least 30 minutes or longer.

Cut pepper and onion into strips. In a large frying pan over medium high heat, brown meat. Add vegetables, except tomato and stir to combine. Sprinkle with fajita seasoning and stir. Continue cooking until tender-crisp. Serve in warm tortillas. Top with tomatoes. Makes 10 (2/3 cup) servings.

Nutrition information: calories 296, calories from fat 121, fat 13 grams, saturated fat 3 grams, cholesterol 61 milligrams, sodium 566 milligrams, carbohydrate 17 grams, fiber 10 gram, sugar 2 gram, protein 25 grams. Exchanges: starch 1, lean meat 3, fat 1/ 2.

Note: This entree may not be appropriate for a low sodium diet.

Flavorful Beef Barbecue

Prep: 10 min   Cook: 6-8 hours

3 pounds London broil, fat trimmed
1/ 2 medium onion, diced
1/2 cup brown sugar
1/2 cup vinegar
3 tablespoons Worcestershire sauce
1 teaspoon mustard
1 can (8 ounces) low sodium tomato sauce
1 teaspoon Accent (or other flavor enhancer)
1 tablespoon garlic powder
1/8 cup lemon juice
1/4 cup water

Preheat oven to 250 degrees.

Place London broil in a 3 1/ 2 to 5-guart slow cooker prepared with nonstick cooking spray. Sprinkle chopped onion over meat. In a 2 quart bowl, combine remaining ingredients. Pour sauce over onions and meat. Cover and cook on low for 6-8 hours or over high for 3-4 hours. Slice thin against grain. Makes 12 servings.

Nutrition information: calories 195, calories from fat 39, total fat 4 grams, saturated fat 1 grams, cholesterol 60 milligrams, sodium 121 milligrams, carbohydrate 13 grams, fiber <1 gram, sugar 10 grams, protein 25 grams. Exchanges: carbohydrate 1, very lean meat 3.

Chicken favorites

A yummy and heart healthy entrée.

Tip: Broiling, baking, and grilling are the healthy ways to cook meat.

Chicken Rollups

Prep: 15 min Cook: 20 min

2 (4 ounces each) boneless skinless chicken breasts
2 tablespoons water
3/4 cup fat free refried beans
1/2 teaspoon onion powder
1/2 teaspoon cumin
1/2 teaspoon garlic powder
1/4 teaspoon chili powder
6 8-inch flour tortillas
4 ounces grated Mexican cheese blend
1/2 cup light sour cream
1 can (4 ounces) green chilies
1 medium tomato, diced

Preheat oven to 350 degrees.

Cut chicken breasts into 1-inch pieces. In a frying pan, cook chicken in water. Drain if necessary and set aside. In a bowl, combine refried beans and seasonings until blended. Spread bean mixture in center of each tortilla. Evenly divide chicken and then cheese, sour cream, chilies, and diced tomato over each tortilla. Roll up and wrap each tortilla in foil. Bake wrapped tortillas for 20 minutes. Makes 6 servings.

Nutrition information: calories 224, calories from fat 67, total fat 7 grams, saturated fat 4 grams, cholesterol 53 milligrams, sodium 532 milligrams, carbohydrate 19 grams, fiber 10 grams, sugar 3 grams, protein 18 grams. Exchanges: starch 1, very lean meat 2, fat 1.

Note: Wheat tortillas may be substituted.

Spicy Chicken and Bean Tacos

Prep: 8 min   Cook: 15 min

4 (4 ounces each) boneless skinless chicken breasts cut into 3/4-
    inch pieces
2 large tomatoes, diced
1 can (15 ounces) spicy chili beans, with sauce
6 medium flour tortillas

Cook chicken in a frying pan prepared with nonstick cooking
spray for about 5 minutes. Add tomatoes and beans. Mix and
reduce heat. Simmer an additional 10 minutes until chicken is
fully cooked. Serve over warm tortillas. Makes 6 servings.

Nutrition information: calories 215, calories from fat 8, total
fat 2 grams, saturated fat <1 gram, sodium 556 milligrams,
carbohydrate 27 grams, fiber 13 grams, sugar 3 grams, protein
24 grams. Exchanges: starch 2, very lean meat 2 1/ 2, vegetables
1/2.

Note: Wheat or corn tortillas may be substituted.

Southwest Chicken Sandwiches

Prep: 8 min   Cook: 45-60 min (if chicken needs to be cooked)

4 whole wheat hamburger buns
8 teaspoons organic bean dip, divided
1/2 cup shredded lettuce
4 (3 ounces each) boneless skinless chicken breasts, fully cooked
1/4 cup chunky salsa, divided
1/2 cup grated mozzarella cheese

Toast hamburger buns. Spread 2 teaspoons of bean dip on each bottom bun. Sprinkle lettuce over bean dip layer. Place a chicken breast over lettuce. Add 1 tablespoon of salsa and then a pinch cheese to the top of each. Makes 4 servings.

Nutrition information: calories 242, calories from fat 92, total fat 10 grams, saturated fat 2 grams, cholesterol 15, sodium 536 milligrams, carbohydrate 22 grams, fiber 2 grams, sugar 2 grams, protein 17 grams. Exchanges: starch 1 1/2, very lean meat 2, fat 2.

Note: Organic bean dip was used in the recipe due to lower sodium content.

Apricot Chicken Delight

Prep: 8 min   Cook: 6-8 hours

6 (4 ounces each) boneless skinless chicken breasts
1/2 cup low sugar apricot preserves
3 tablespoons brown sugar
1 cup water
2 tablespoons cornstarch

Place chicken in a 5- to 7-quart slow cooker prepared with nonstick cooking spray. Combine remaining ingredients except cornstarch. Cover and cook on low for 6–8 hours. Drain liquid into a sauce pan and boil with cornstarch to thicken. Place chicken on a serving platter and drizzle sauce over the top. Makes 6 servings.

Nutrition information: calories 237, calories from fat 18, total fat 2 grams, saturated fat <1 gram, cholesterol 65 milligrams, sodium 80 milligrams, carbohydrate 25 grams, fiber 0 grams, sugar 16 grams, protein 26 grams. Exchanges: starch 2, very lean meat 3 1/2.

Ranch Baked Chicken

Prep: 6 min   Bake: 35 min

1/3 cup Italian-style breadcrumbs
2 tablespoons grated Parmesan cheese
4 (4 ounces each) boneless skinless chicken breasts
1/4 cup light ranch dressing

Preheat oven to 350 degrees.

Combine breadcrumbs and cheese. Dip chicken into ranch dressing and then roll in breadcrumb mixture. Place chicken on a baking sheet prepared with nonstick cooking spray. Bake for 35 minutes. Makes 4 servings.

Nutrition information: calories 231, calories from fat 79, total fat 8 grams, saturated fat 2 gram, cholesterol 69 milligrams, sodium 342 milligrams, carbohydrate 8 grams, sugar 1 gram, fiber <1 gram, protein 28 grams. Exchanges: starch 1/2, very lean meat 3 1/2, fat 1.

Easy Lemon Chicken

Prep: 6 min   Cook: 15-20 min

6 (4 ounces each) boneless skinless chicken breasts
2 tablespoons butter or margarine
1/2 cup chicken broth
1/2 teaspoon dill weed
1 tablespoon lemon juice
1/2 teaspoon salt

In a frying pan, cook chicken in butter for 5 minutes. In a separate bowl, combine broth, dill weed, lemon juice, and salt. Pour over chicken and cook an additional 10 minutes or until juices run clear. Remove chicken from pan. Boil mixture until reduced to half. Pour over chicken. Makes 6 servings.

Nutrition information: calories 143, calories from fat 31, total fat 3 grams, saturated fat 1 gram, cholesterol 69 milligrams, sodium 164 milligrams, carbohydrate <1 gram, fiber <1 gram, sugar <1 gram, protein 26 grams. Exchanges: very lean meat 3 1/2.

Southwestern Style Lasagna

Prep: 15 min   Cook: 30 min

2 cans (10.5 ounces each) reduced fat cream of chicken soup,
    condensed
2 medium tomatoes, diced
1/2 can (4 ounces) diced green chilies
1 teaspoon garlic powder
1 teaspoon onion powder
1 teaspoon cumin
1/2 teaspoon chili powder
6 medium tortillas, torn into thin strips, divided
3 (4 ounces each) boneless skinless chicken breasts,
    cooked and diced
1 cup grated Mexican cheese blend

Preheat oven to 350 degrees.

In a medium bowl, combine soup, tomatoes, chilies, and seasonings.
Place 1/3 of tortilla pieces in bottom of a 9 x 13-inch baking dish
prepared with nonstick cooking spray. Place half of chicken on
top of tortilla pieces. Follow with half of soup mixture. Repeat
layers and top with remaining tortilla pieces. Cover and bake for
30 minutes. Sprinkle cheese on top for last 3 minutes of baking
time. Makes 8 servings.

Nutrition information: calories 187, calories from fat 34, total fat
4 grams, saturated fat 2 gram, cholesterol 38 milligrams, sodium
504 milligrams, carbohydrate 20 grams, fiber 8 grams, protein 16
grams. Exchanges: starch 1, very lean meat 2.

Note: Wheat or corn tortillas may be substituted.

Western Chicken Pizza

Prep: 10 min Cook: 10 min

2 tablespoons barbecue sauce
2 tablespoons water
1 (12-inch, 12 ounces) pre-baked pizza crust
2 (4 ounces each) boneless skinless chicken breasts, cooked
1 cup grated mozzarella cheese
2 tablespoons diced red onion
8-ounce package pre-sliced fresh mushrooms

Preheat oven to 425 degrees.

Mix barbecue sauce with water. Evenly spread barbecue sauce mixture over pizza crust. Shred chicken and then arrange over pizza. Sprinkle cheese over chicken. Place onion and mushrooms over top. Bake 10 minutes until cheese is melted and pizza is hot. Makes 8 servings.

Nutrition information: calories 365, calories from fat 103, total fat 11 grams, saturated fat <1 gram, cholesterol 85 milligrams, sodium 696 milligrams, carbohydrate 21 grams, fiber <1 gram, sugar <1 gram, protein 44 grams. Exchanges: starch 1 1/2, very lean meat 6, fat 2.

Note: This item may not be appropriate for a low sodium diet.

Darin's Parmesan Chicken Pizza

Prep: 6 min   Cook: 3-5 min

3/4 cup Parmesan and mozzarella cheese sauce
1-12 inch loaf wheat French bread cut in half horizontally
2 (4 ounces each) boneless skinless chicken breasts, cooked and
    sliced
8 ounce package pre-sliced fresh mushrooms
1 cup grated mozzarella cheese
2 tablespoons grated Parmesan cheese

Preheat broiler.

Spread cheese sauce evenly over both slices of bread. Arrange chicken and mushrooms on top of sauce. Sprinkle cheeses over top. Broil until cheese is melted and starts to brown. Makes 8 servings.

Nutrition information: calories 222, calories from fat 72, total fat 7 grams, saturated fat 3 grams, cholesterol 33 milligrams, sodium 424 milligrams, carbohydrate 23 grams, fiber 3 grams, sugar 4 grams, protein 15 grams. Exchanges: starch 1 1/2, very lean meat 2, fat 1/2.

Baked Italian Chicken

Prep: 7 min   Cook: 40 min

2 pounds boneless skinless chicken tenders
4 ounces pre-sliced fresh mushrooms
1 cup reduced sugar spaghetti sauce
1/2 cup grated mozzarella cheese
4 tablespoons grated Parmesan cheese

Preheat oven to 350 degrees.

In a 9 x 13 baking dish prepared with nonstick cooking spray, arrange chicken and mushrooms. Cover and cook for 30 minutes. Remove from oven and pour sauce over all. Sprinkle cheeses over top. Return to oven and bake 5–10 minutes until cheese is bubbly. Makes 8 servings.

Nutrition information: calories 96, calories from fat 30, total fat 3 grams, saturated fat <1 gram, cholesterol 24 milligrams, sodium 237 milligrams, carbohydrate 4 grams, fiber 1 gram, sugar 1 gram, protein 12 grams. Exchanges: very lean meat 1 1/2.

Glazed Chicken

Prep: 5 min   Cook: 6-10 min

2 tablespoons honey Dijon mustard
3 tablespoons brown sugar
1 tablespoon honey
1/4 teaspoon ginger
1 tablespoon hot water
1 pound boneless skinless chicken tenders

Preheat broiler.

In a small bowl, combine mustard, sugar, honey, ginger, and water. Stir well. Place chicken pieces on a baking sheet prepared with nonstick cooking spray. Divide glaze in half. Brush half on chicken pieces. Broil 3–5 minutes. Turn chicken breasts and brush remaining glaze on other side. Continue to broil until juices run clear and glaze becomes sticky on chicken. Makes 4 servings.

Nutrition information: calories 198, calories from fat 25, total fat 3 grams, saturated fat <1 gram, cholesterol 65 milligrams, sodium 253 milligrams, carbohydrate 14 grams, fiber <1 gram, sugar 14 grams, protein 26 grams. Exchanges: carbohydrate 1, very lean meat 3.

Marinara Parmesan Chicken

Prep: 5 min   Cook: 8 min

1/2 cup Italian breadcrumbs
2 tablespoons grated Parmesan cheese
1/4 cup egg substitute
1 pound boneless skinless chicken breasts cut into strips
1 cup spaghetti sauce
1/4 cup grated mozzarella cheese

In a small bowl, combine breadcrumbs and Parmesan cheese. Place egg substitute in another small bowl. Dip chicken pieces into egg and then roll in bread crumbs to coat. Cook in large frying pan prepared with nonstick cooking spray. Cook 7–8 minutes or until center of chicken is no longer pink. In another 2 quart sauce pan, heat spaghetti sauce until slightly bubbly. Spoon sauce and sprinkle cheese evenly over chicken. Makes 6 servings.

Nutritional information: calories 129, calories from fat 44, total fat 3 grams, saturated fat 2 grams, fiber <1 gram, cholesterol 21 milligrams, sodium 506 milligrams, carbohydrate 16 grams, fiber <1 gram, sugar 4 grams, protein 11 grams. Exchanges: carbohydrate 1, very lean meat 1 1/2.

Orange Peanut Butter Chicken

Prep: 8 min   Cook: 30 min

1/4 cup orange juice
2 tablespoons reduced fat peanut butter
1/2 tablespoon low sodium soy sauce
1/2 teaspoon ground ginger
1 1/2 pounds boneless skinless chicken tenders or breasts

Preheat oven to 400 degrees.

In a gallon size re-sealable plastic bag, combine orange juice, peanut butter, soy sauce, and ginger. Seal bag and shake or squeeze in hands until sauce is smooth. Add chicken. Close bag and work in hands to coat all chicken pieces with sauce. Arrange coated chicken in a 9 x 13-inch baking dish prepared with nonstick cooking spray. Cover and bake for 30 minutes. Makes 6 servings.

Nutrition information: calories 77, calories from fat 22, total fat 2 grams, saturated fat <1 gram, cholesterol 20 milligrams, sodium 99 milligrams, carbohydrate 4 grams, fiber <1 gram, sugar 2 grams, protein 9 grams. Exchange: very lean meat 1.

White Pasta Chicken

Prep: 5 min   Cook: 12 min

1 box (14.5 ounces) penne pasta
1 pound boneless skinless chicken breasts
1 cup reduced sodium chicken broth
1 jar (16 ounces) garlic Alfredo sauce
1 tablespoon soft bacon bits
2 medium Roma tomatoes, diced

Cook pasta according to package directions. In a 6-quart saucepan, cook chicken in broth. Break into pieces as it cooks. Add Alfredo sauce, bacon bits, and tomatoes. Reduce heat to low and cook until heated through. Stir drained cooked pasta into chicken mixture. Serve immediately. Makes 11 (1 cup) servings.

Nutrition information: calories 246, calories from fat 51, total fat 5 grams, saturated fat 3 grams, cholesterol 36 milligrams , sodium 216 milligrams, carbohydrate 32 grams, fiber <1 gram, sugar 3 grams, protein 17 grams. Exchanges: starch 2, very lean meat 2, fat 1/2.

Note: Whole wheat or whole grain pasta can be substituted.

Honey Chicken Legs

Prep: 25 min Cook: 30 min

2 teaspoons onion powder
1 teaspoon ground chili powder
2 teaspoons garlic powder
1 teaspoon pepper
2 teaspoons seasoned salt
14 chicken legs, skinned
1/2 cup honey
1/4 cup barbecue sauce
1 teaspoon liquid smoke

Combine onion powder, chili powder, garlic powder, pepper, and seasoned salt. Rub seasonings onto chicken legs. Arrange chicken legs in a 9 x 13-inch baking dish prepared with nonstick cooking spray. Let chicken legs dry for 20 minutes.

Preheat oven to 350 degrees. Cover pan with aluminum foil and bake for 30 minutes. Remove from oven and pour off all but 3 tablespoons of liquid. Combine reserved liquid, honey, barbecue sauce, and liquid smoke. Drizzle over legs. Cover and return to oven for 20 minutes. Makes 14 servings.

Nutrition information: calories 136, calories from fat 29, total fat 3 grams, saturated fat <1 gram, cholesterol 62 milligrams, sodium 321 milligrams, carbohydrate 10 grams, fiber <1 gram, sugar 9 grams, protein 16 grams. Exchanges: starch 1 /2, very lean meat 2.

Seasoned Turkey

Prep: 7 min   Bake: 2 hours

3 pounds turkey breast, skinned
1/2 teaspoon garlic powder
1/2 teaspoon onion powder
1/2 teaspoon sage
1/2 teaspoon thyme
1/8 teaspoon pepper

Preheat oven to 350 degrees.

Wash turkey under cold water. Pat dry with a paper towel and place in a 9 x 13-inch baking dish prepared with nonstick cooking spray. Mix seasonings together and rub onto turkey breast. Cover and cook for 2 hours or until cooked through. Makes 12 servings.

Nutrition information: calories 163, calories from fat 72, total fat 3 grams, saturated fat 2 grams, cholesterol 65 milligrams, sodium 200 milligrams, carbohydrate <1 gram, fiber <1 gram, sugar 0 grams, protein 22 grams. Exchanges: very lean meat 3.

Note: Make gravy from the drippings if desired.

Cold Turkey Sandwiches

Prep: 8 min

4 cups coleslaw cabbage and carrot salad
1/4 cup minced onion
1/4 teaspoon Italian seasoning
1 cup fat free mayonnaise, divided
12 whole wheat rolls
2 pounds cooked shredded turkey
2 medium tomatoes, sliced
1 medium cucumber, sliced

In a medium bowl, mix coleslaw, onion, Italian seasoning, and 1/2 cup mayonnaise until blended. Set aside. Slice each roll in half, brushing both halves with remaining mayonnaise. Arrange turkey, tomato, and cucumber on sandwiches. Top with coleslaw mixture. Wrap in foil to hold together or eat as is. Works well with hot or cold turkey. Makes 12 servings.

Nutrition information: calories 210, calories from fat 65, total fat 4 grams, saturated fat 1 gram, cholesterol 43 milligrams, sodium 396 milligrams, carbohydrate 18 grams, fiber 2 grams, sugar 5 grams, protein 17 grams. Exchanges: starch 1, very lean meat 2.

Variation: Add a slice of your favorite cheese.

Pork and Seafood entrees

Not your mammas' pork and seafood!

Tip: On the food label, the % daily value for fat is a quick way to determine if the food is heart healthy. If it is 5% or less, the item is low in fat, saturated fat, cholesterol, and trans-fat.

Spiced Maple Ham

Prep: 2 min   Cook: 15 min

1 pound low sodium ham steaks, fully cooked
1/2 cup light maple syrup
1 teaspoon ground cloves
1/2 teaspoon ground cinnamon
1/4 to 1/2 cup water

Place ham steaks in a frying pan over medium heat. Combine remaining ingredients and pour over ham. Cover and simmer for 15 minutes. Collect remaining syrup mixture and serve with ham. Makes 5 servings.

Nutrition information: calories 127, calories from fat 17, total fat 2 grams, saturated fat <1 gram, cholesterol 35 milligrams, sodium 688 milligrams, carbohydrate 15 grams, fiber <1 gram, sugar 9 grams, protein 12 grams. Exchanges: carbohydrate 1, lean meat 1 1/2.

Note: This entrée may not be appropriate for a low sodium diet.

Dijon Glazed Ham Kabobs

Prep: 15 min Cook: 5 min

1/4 cup honey
3 tablespoons Dijon mustard
1 clove garlic, minced
1 medium red bell pepper
1 pound thick ham slices, from deli
20 snow pea pods
1 can (20 ounces) pineapple chunks, drained
12 fresh mushrooms

Bamboo sticks should be soaked in water for one hour prior to using to prevent from charring or catching on fire.

Combine honey, mustard, and garlic. Set aside. Cut bell pepper into chunks and ham into 1-inch squares. Wrap snow pea pods around pineapple and thread onto 6 bamboo sticks alternating with bell pepper, ham, and mushrooms until all are used. Brush honey mixture on kabobs and grill or broil about 5 minutes or until heated through. Turn kabobs and brush with remaining honey mixture. Cook an additional 1–2 minutes. Makes 6 servings.

Nutrition information: calories 195, calories from fat 23, total fat 6 grams, saturated fat <1 gram, cholesterol 42 milligrams, sodium 767 milligrams, carbohydrate 24 grams, fiber 1 gram, sugar 19 grams, protein 17 grams. Exchanges: fruit 1/2, lean meat 2, vegetable 1.

Note: This entrée may not be appropriate for a low sodium diet.

Grilled Seasoned Pork Chops

Prep: 3 min plus marinate time   Cook: 7 min

1/2 cup balsamic vinegar
1/4 cup olive oil
3 cloves garlic, minced
1 teaspoon dried sage
1 teaspoon dried thyme
1 teaspoon dried rosemary
1 tablespoon dried parsley
1 1/2 pounds (6 count) boneless pork sirloin cutlets

Blend vinegar, olive oil, garlic, sage, thyme, rosemary, and parsley in a blender. Place cutlets in a 9 x 13-inch glass baking dish. Pour seasoning marinade over cutlets. Cover and marinate for at least 3 hours or overnight. Grill marinated cutlets over medium high heat 5–7 minutes on each side until done. Makes 6 servings.

Nutritional information: calories 262, calories from fat 141, total fat 15 grams, saturated fat 3 grams, cholesterol 74 milligrams, sodium 363 milligrams, carbohydrate 6 grams, fiber <1 gram, sugar 5 grams, protein 23 grams. Exchanges: medium fat meat 3.

Tasty Pork

Prep: 3 min   Cook: 1 hour

1 pound (4 count) boneless pork sirloin cutlets
2 tablespoons ketchup
3 tablespoons honey
2 tablespoons vinegar
1 teaspoon ground thyme
1/2 teaspoon mustard
1 tablespoon water

Preheat oven to 350 degrees.

Arrange pork cutlets in a 9 x 13-inch baking pan prepared with nonstick cooking spray. Mix remaining ingredients and pour over pork. Cover and bake at 350 for 1 hour. Makes 4 servings.

Nutrition information: calories 216, calories from fat 58, total fat 9, saturated fat 2 grams, cholesterol 74 milligrams, sodium 164 milligrams, carbohydrate 14 grams, fiber <1 gram, sugar 14 grams, protein 23 grams. Exchanges: carbohydrate 1, medium fat meat 3.

Orange Glazed Pork

Prep: 3 min   Cook: 1 hour

2 pounds (8 count) boneless pork sirloin cutlets
1 1/2 teaspoons Worcestershire sauce
1/2 teaspoon garlic powder
Dash pepper
1 can (6 ounces) orange juice concentrate

Preheat oven to 350 degrees.

Arrange pork cutlets in a 9 x 13-inch baking dish prepared with nonstick cooking spray. Mix remaining ingredients in a bowl and pour over pork. Cover and bake for 1 hour. Makes 8 servings.

Nutrition information: calories 200, calories from fat 57, total fat 9 grams, saturated fat 2 grams, cholesterol 75 milligrams, sodium 70 milligrams, carbohydrate 11 grams, fiber <1 gram, sugar 10 grams, protein 23 grams. Exchanges: fruit 1, lean meat 3.

Pork Soft Tacos

Prep: 5 min   Cook: 1 hour

3 pounds pork roast, trimmed
1/4 cup vinegar
3 tablespoons olive oil
2 tablespoons steak sauce
2 cloves garlic, minced
1/2 teaspoon savory
1/2 teaspoon dry mustard
12 6-inch tortillas

For salsa:
1/2 large onion, finely chopped
1 cup chopped cilantro
2 tomatillos, cored, diced
1 tablespoon jalapeño, seeded and diced
1/2 teaspoon salt
2 cloves garlic, minced
1/2 medium lime

Cut pork roast into steak-size pieces. In a re-sealable plastic bag, combine vinegar, oil, steak sauce, garlic, savory, and mustard. Seal bag and mix contents with hands. Add cut pork steaks and marinate at least 4 hours in the refrigerator. Mix occasionally to spread marinade. Grill for 7–9 minutes on each side, turning once, until juices run clear. In a small bowl, combine all salsa ingredients except lime. Squeeze juice from lime over salsa. Cover and let set until meat is marinated and cooked. After meat is cooked, transfer to cutting board. Slice into small bite-size pieces. Serve immediately, folded into warm tortillas. Garnish with salsa. Makes 12 servings.

Nutrition information: calories 237, calories from fat 75, total fat 7 grams, saturated fat 2 grams, cholesterol 73 milligrams, sodium 263 milligrams, carbohydrate 13 grams, fiber 9 gram, sugar <1 gram, protein 25 grams. Exchanges: Starch 1, very lean meat 3, fat 1/2.

Note: Tomatillos are found in the refrigerated produce section. They look like green tomatoes covered with leaves and are sticky to the touch.

Honey Mustard Garlic Pork

Prep: 3 min   Cook: 1 hour

1 cup reduced sodium beef broth
1/2 cup honey mustard
2 garlic cloves, minced
1 1/2 pounds (6 count) boneless pork sirloin cutlets

Preheat oven to 350 degrees.

Mix together broth, honey mustard, and garlic. Remove all visible fat from meat. In a 9 x 13-inch baking pan prepared with nonstick cooking spray, arrange pork pieces. Pour honey mustard mixture over top and bake, uncovered, for 1 hour. Makes 6 servings.

Nutrition information: calories 289, calories from fat 111, total fat 12 grams, saturated fat 4 grams, cholesterol 98 milligrams, sodium 198 milligrams, carbohydrate 8 grams, fiber <1 gram, sugar 4 grams, protein 30 grams. Exchanges: carbohydrate 1/2, lean meat 4.

Saucy Pork Chops

Prep: 3 min plus 30 for marinate   Cook: 50 min

1/2 cup ketchup
1/2 cup water
2 tablespoons vinegar
1 tablespoon Worcestershire sauce
2 tablespoons brown sugar
1/4 teaspoon seasoned salt
1/2 teaspoon chili powder
1/8 teaspoon pepper
2 pounds (8 count) pork loin cutlets

Preheat oven to 350 degrees.

In a plastic re-sealable bag combine all ingredients except cutlets. Seal bag and mix with hands until blended, and then add pork. Marinate for at least 30 minutes. Carefully pour all ingredients into a 9 x 13-inch baking dish prepared with nonstick cooking spray. Arrange pork so that it is lying flat and in a single layer. Cover and bake for 50 minutes. Serve immediately with sauce leftover in the baking dish. Makes 8 servings.

Nutrition information: calories 184, calories from fat 56, total fat 9 grams, saturated fat 2 grams, cholesterol 74 milligrams, sodium 317 milligrams, carbohydrate 7 grams, fiber <1 gram, sugar 7 grams, protein 23 grams. Exchanges: lean meat 3, other carbohydrate 1/2.

Marmalade Barbecue Pork Chops

Prep: 2 min   Cook: 10 min

1/4 cup honey barbecue sauce
1/4 cup sugar free orange marmalade
1 1/2 pounds (8 count) pork sirloin chops, 1/2-inch thick

In a small bowl, mix together barbecue sauce and marmalade until blended. Place pork on heated grill. Cook about 5 minutes on each side or until juices run clear. Turn only once. As the first side cooks, brush with barbecue mixture. Continue with second side. Makes 8 servings.

Nutrition information: calories 215, calories from fat 86, total fat 9 grams, saturated fat 3 grams, cholesterol 73 milligrams, sodium 116 milligrams, carbohydrate 7 grams, fiber <1 gram, sugar 7 grams, protein 25 grams. Exchanges: carbohydrate 1 /2, very lean meat 3.

Caramelized Pork

Prep: 8 min   Cook: 16 min

2 pounds (8 count) thin cut boneless pork chops
1 tablespoon olive oil
1 teaspoon seasoned salt
1/4 teaspoon pepper
1/2 medium red onion, sliced and separated
2 cloves garlic, minced
4 ounces fresh pre-sliced mushrooms
3 tablespoons orange juice
4 tablespoons brown sugar
1/4 cup water

In a large frying pan, brown pork chops in oil for 10 minutes over medium heat. Sprinkle with seasoned salt and pepper. Add onion and garlic. Turn pork to mix and cook onion until tender-crisp. Add mushrooms and continue turning pork until fully cooked. In a small bowl, mix together orange juice and brown sugar until sugar is dissolved. Add to pork and stir to coat. Pour water over top. Reduce heat and cover, simmering 5–6 minutes. Serve immediately with mushrooms and onions placed on top of pork. Makes 8 servings.

Nutrition information: calories 241, calories from fat 114, total fat 15 grams, saturated fat 4 grams, cholesterol 59 milligrams, sodium 622 milligrams, carbohydrate 10 grams, fiber <1 gram, sugar 8 grams, protein 22 grams. Exchanges: carbohydrate 1 /2, lean meat 3 1/2.

Note: This entrée may not be appropriate for a low sodium diet.

Creamy Pork and Potato Dinner

Prep: 10 min Cook: 1 hour

1 pound baby carrots, halved
1 pound red potatoes, quartered
8 ounce package pre-sliced fresh mushrooms
1/3 cup diced onion
1 tablespoon Italian seasoning
1 1/2 pounds (8 count) thin cut boneless pork loin chops
1 can (10.5 ounce) reduced fat cream of mushroom soup,
   condensed

Preheat oven to 350 degrees.

Place carrots, potatoes, mushrooms, and onion in a 9 x 13-inch baking dish prepared with nonstick cooking spray. Sprinkle Italian seasoning over top. Lay cutlets evenly over vegetables. Spread soup over pork chops. Cover and bake for 1 hour 15 minutes or until vegetables are tender. Makes 8 servings.

Nutrition information: calories 258, calories from fat 130, total fat 14 grams, saturated fat <1 gram, cholesterol 1 milligram, sodium 216 milligrams, carbohydrate 13 grams, fiber 3 grams, sugar 4 grams, protein 18 grams. Exchanges: starch 1, lean meat 2 1/2, vegetable 1, fat 1 /2.

Romano Crusted Tilapia

Prep: 4 min   Cook: 35 min

1/3 cup Italian-style breadcrumbs
2 tablespoons grated Romano cheese
1 tablespoon crushed red pepper flakes
1 teaspoon onion powder
4 (4 ounces each) tilapia fillets
1/4 cup light ranch dressing

Preheat oven to 350 degrees.

Combine breadcrumbs, cheese, onion powder, and red pepper flakes. Dip fish fillets into ranch dressing to coat and then roll into breadcrumb mixture. Place fish on a baking sheet prepared with nonstick cooking spray. Bake for 35 minutes. Makes 4 servings.

Nutrition information: calories 227, calories from fat 93, total fat 10 grams, saturated fat <1 gram, cholesterol 70 milligrams, sodium 434 milligrams, carbohydrate 9 grams, fiber <1 gram, sugar 1 gram, protein 23 grams. Exchanges: lean meat 3, fat 1/2.

Shrimp Stir-Fry

Prep: 10 min Cook: 12-15 min

2 cloves garlic
1 tablespoon olive oil
1/2 pound frozen cooked salad shrimp, cleaned and peeled
1 bag (16 ounces) frozen stir-fry vegetables
8 ounce package pre-sliced fresh mushrooms
1/4 cup stir-fry sauce
1/4 cup hot water

Crush garlic cloves and add to oil in a large frying pan. Cook until tender. Add shrimp, vegetables, and mushrooms to garlic. Cook until heated through. Add stir-fry sauce and hot water. Cook an additional 2–3 minutes, stirring to coat. Makes 6 (1 cup) servings.

Nutrition information: calories 86, calories from fat 20, total fat 2 grams, saturated fat <1 gram, cholesterol 42 milligrams, sodium 467 milligrams, carbohydrate 10 grams, fiber 2 grams, sugar 4 grams, protein 7 grams. Exchanges: starch 1, very lean meat 1, vegetable 2.

Fettuccine Pasta with Shrimp

Prep: 5 min   Cook: 15 min

1 package (13.25 ounces) fettuccine noodles
3/4 cup frozen peas
8 ounces frozen salad shrimp, peeled and tails removed
1 jar (16 ounces) Alfredo sauce
1 cup skim milk
1/4 teaspoon black pepper
1 large Roma tomato, diced

In a large pot, boil pasta following directions on the package. In a medium saucepan, cook shrimp until heated through. Add peas, Alfredo sauce, milk, and pepper until heated. Stir in tomatoes. Mix together with noodles. Makes 10(1 cup) servings.

Nutrition information: calories 231, calories from fat 54, total fat 6 grams, saturated fat 2 grams, cholesterol 40 milligrams, sodium 335 milligrams, carbohydrates 35 grams, fiber <1 gram, sugar 5 grams, protein 10 grams. Exchanges: starch 2, very lean meat 1, fat 1/2.

Note: Wheat noodles may be substituted.

Shrimp Primavera Pasta

Prep: 5 min   Cook: 15 min

1 box (16 ounces) spaghetti noodles
1/2 cup onion, diced
2 cloves garlic, pressed
1 tablespoon olive oil
8 ounce package pre-sliced fresh mushrooms
1 can (26 ounces) reduced sugar spaghetti sauce
6 ounce frozen cooked salad shrimp, cooked

Cook noodles according to package directions. In a saucepan, combine onion, garlic, and olive oil. Sauté until onions are tender-crisp. Add mushrooms and spaghetti sauce. Add shrimp to spaghetti sauce and simmer for 5 minutes until heated through. Combine noodles and sauce. Makes 8 (1 cup) servings.

Nutrition information: calories: 373, calories from fat 51, total fat 7 grams, saturated fat 1 gram, cholesterol <1 milligrams, sodium 468 milligrams, carbohydrate 42 grams, fiber 4 grams sugar 9 grams, protein 14 grams. Exchanges: starch 2 1/2, very lean meat 1 1/2, fat 1.

Note: Wheat or whole grain noodles may be substituted.

Delicious desserts: all around 30 carbohydrates

So good it's always worth it.

Tip: Too much of a good thing is a disaster for you blood glucose. Limiting portions is one way to keep blood sugar in check.

Lemon Poppy Seed Bundt Cake

Prep: 6 min   Cook: 50 min

1 lemon cake mix (18.25 ounces)
1/4 cup unsweetened applesauce
8 egg whites or 4 egg substitute equivalents
1 cup fat free sour cream
2 teaspoons lemon extract
1 tablespoon poppy seeds

Preheat oven to 350 degrees.

Combine all ingredients together in a large bowl. Beat for 1–2 minutes. Bake in a bundt pan prepared generously with nonstick cooking spray for 45–50 minutes. Store covered in the refrigerator. Makes 16 servings.

Nutrition information: calories 157, calories from fat 26, fat 3 grams, saturated fat <1 gram, cholesterol 10 milligrams, sodium 274 milligrams, carbohydrate 28 grams, fiber <1 gram, sugar 15 grams, protein 4 grams. Exchanges: carbohydrate 2.

Cookie Cheesecake

Prep: 6 min   Chill: 4 hours

1 package (8 ounces) fat free cream cheese, softened
1 box (1.34 ounce) sugar free vanilla pudding mix
3 tablespoons skim milk
1 cup crushed reduced fat chocolate sandwich cookies, divided
1 container (8 ounces) frozen light or sugar free whipped
    topping, thawed

In a large bowl, beat cream cheese, pudding, and milk until smooth. Fold in 1/3 cup crushed cookies and then whipped topping. In an 11 x 7-inch baking dish, arrange about 1/3 cup of crushed cookies on bottom of pan. Spoon cream cheese mixture onto crushed cookies and evenly spread. Chill 4 hours. Top with remaining cookie crumbs just before serving. Refrigerate any leftovers. Makes 8 servings.

Nutrition information: calories 214, calories from 68 , total fat 7 grams, saturated fat 5 grams, cholesterol 5 milligrams, sodium 351 milligrams, carbohydrate 28 grams, fiber 1 gram, sugar 13 grams, protein 4 grams. Exchanges: carbohydrate 2, fat 1.

Apple Pie Cake

Prep: 5 min   Cook: 40 min

1 reduced sugar yellow or white cake mix (18.25 ounces)
1 1/2 cups uncooked quick oats
1 teaspoon cinnamon
1/2 teaspoon nutmeg
1/2 cup brown sugar, divided
1/2 cup unsweetened applesauce
3/4 cup skim milk
1 can (20 ounces) low sugar apple pie filling

Preheat oven to 350 degrees.

Combine cake mix, oats, cinnamon, and nutmeg. Add in brown sugar, minus 1 tablespoon held in reserve. Mix until well blended. Stir in applesauce, milk, and pie filling. Spread batter evenly in a 9 x 13-inch pan prepared with nonstick cooking spray. Sprinkle remaining brown sugar on top. Bake for 35–40 minutes. Makes 24 servings.

Nutrition information: calories 183, calories from fat 48, total fat 5 grams, saturated fat 1 gram, cholesterol 27 milligrams, sodium 158 milligrams, carbohydrate 30 grams, fiber <1 gram, sugar 18 grams, protein 3 grams. Exchanges: starch 1, fruit 1, fat 1.

Note: Top with whipped topping if desired.

Apple Pie Turnovers

Prep: 15 min Cook: 8 min

1 can (20 ounces) light apple pie filling
1/2 teaspoon cinnamon
1/2 teaspoon nutmeg
8 phyllo pastry sheets
1 tablespoon sugar

Preheat oven to 375 degrees.

In a medium bowl, mix pie filling and spices. Slightly chop apple pieces to a smaller size. Follow directions on package of phyllo pastry to prevent sheets from drying. Lay out 4 pastry sheets, spraying with nonstick cooking spray. Repeat with remaining sheets. Cut each lengthwise in half, using a pizza cuter. Place 1 1/2 tablespoon apple mixture onto one end of the strip. Fold corner over into a triangle. Continue folding like a flag until complete. Continue with remaining ingredients. Place on a baking sheet sprayed with nonstick cooking spray. Bake for 8 minutes until golden brown. Remove and sprinkle with sugar. Makes 12 servings.

Variation: Low sugar cherries or blueberries can be substituted.

Nutrition information: calories 96, calories from fat 2, total fat <1 gram, saturated fat <1 gram, cholesterol 0 milligrams, sodium 51 milligrams, carbohydrate 22 grams, fiber <1 gram, sugar 6 grams, protein 1 gram. Exchanges: fruit 1.

Strawberry Brownie Dessert

Prep: 12 min Prep: 25 min

1 large box (19.8 ounces) brownie mix
1/4 cup water
1/4 cup baby food prune puree
1/2 cup egg substitute
1/4 cup sugar free chocolate ice cream syrup, divided
2 tablespoons caramel ice cream topping
1 container (8 ounces) frozen light or sugar free whipped
    topping, thawed
2 cups fresh or frozen strawberries

Preheat oven to 350 degrees.

In a large bowl, combine brownie mix, water, prune puree, and egg substitute. Pour batter into a 9 x 13-inch baking pan prepared with nonstick cooking spray. Bake for 25 minutes or until a toothpick comes out clean when pricked. Let cool. Drizzle 2 tablespoons chocolate syrup and caramel topping over brownies. Spread whipped topping over syrup. Slice strawberries and arrange over top. Drizzle with remaining chocolate syrup. Store covered in refrigerator. Makes 18 servings.

Nutrition information: calories 175, calories from fat 53, total fat 6 grams, saturated fat 2 grams, cholesterol 0 milligrams, sodium 111 milligrams, carbohydrates 28 grams, fiber 1 gram, sugar 19, protein 2 grams. Exchanges: carbohydrate 2, fat 1.

Note: Prune puree will intensify the chocolate flavor in the brownies and keeps them moist. Pureed prunes can be found in the baby food section of the grocery store already pre-measured.

Brownie Delight

Prep: 10 min Bake: time varies

1 large (19.8 ounce) brownie mix
2 egg whites
¼ cup prune puree
2 (8 ounce) sugar free whipped topping
1(6 ounce) Sugar free vanilla yogurt
1 small (1.5 ounce) sugar free chocolate pudding mix
1 cup skim milk

Make brownie mix according to package directions substituting 2 egg whites for one whole egg. Use pureed prune in place of oil. Bake and let cool. Cut into bite size pieces. Mix yogurt and one container of whipped topping until blended. Mix pudding using one cup skim milk and 1 cup cold water. In small serving bowls equally spoon yogurt mixture into bottom of bowl. Top with brownie pieces, pudding, and whipped topping. Make 18 servings.

Nutrition information: Calories 217, calories from fat 67, total fat 7 grams, saturated fat 3 grams, cholesterol <1 milligram, sodium 113 milligrams, carbohydrate 34 grams, fiber <1 gram, sugar 22 grams, protein 2 grams. Exchanges: fat 1, other carbohydrate 1 ½.

Chocolate Graham Balls

Prep: 20 min plus refrigeration

12 whole graham crackers
2 cups frozen light whipped topping, thawed
3/4 cup reduced fat creamy peanut butter
1 cup powdered sugar
1 1/2 cups chocolate chips

Finely crush graham crackers and set aside. In a large bowl, mix peanut butter, whipped topping, and powdered sugar. Add crushed graham crackers. Continue stirring until uniformly mixed. Roll into 40 balls 1 inch in diameter. Refrigerate until firm. Melt chocolate chips on a microwave safe dinner plate. Heat chocolate chips 30 seconds at a time. Roll graham balls in chocolate with a fork until coated. Remove to waxed paper. Allow to chocolate coating to harden in refrigerator. Store covered in refrigerator. Makes 20 servings (2 balls per serving).

Note: For quicker hardening of chocolate put in freezer for 10 min.

Nutrition information: calories 191, calories from fat 76, total fat 8 grams, saturated fat 4 grams, cholesterol 2 milligrams, sodium 105 milligrams, carbohydrate 25 grams, fiber 1 gram, sugar 7 grams, protein 3 grams. Exchanges: carbohydrate 2, fat 1 1/2.

Dessert Breadsticks

Prep: 5 min   Cook: time varies

1 tube low fat refrigerated breadsticks
¼ teaspoon cinnamon
1 tablespoon brown sugar
Butter flavored nonstick cooking spray
¼ cup powdered sugar
1 ½ teaspoons skim milk
¼ teaspoon vanilla

Unroll breadsticks from package. With a pizza cutter, cut each bread stick into thirds. Mix cinnamon and brown sugar in a large bowl. Spray one side of breadsticks with butter flavored spray. Lay prepared side of breadstick facedown in sugar mixture. Twist bread stick and pull slightly longer as you place on a baking sheet prepared with nonstick cooking spray. Continue until all are done. Bake according to package directions. While breadsticks are cooking, mix powdered sugar, milk, and vanilla. Drizzle on breadsticks. Makes 12 servings. (2 sticks each)

Nutrition information: calories 42, calories from fat 5, total fat <1 gram, saturated fat <1 gram, cholesterol <1 gram, sodium 44 milligrams, carbohydrate 8 grams, fiber <1 gram, sugar 3 grams, protein 2 grams. Exchanges: 1/2 starch.

Variation: Omit glaze and dip sticks into light vanilla yogurt or sugar free whipped topping.

Cinnamon and Sugar Pull-a-parts

Prep: 5 min   Bake: time varies

Butter flavored nonstick cooking spray
2 packages (7.5 ounces each) reduced fat refrigerated biscuits
2 tablespoons sugar
½ teaspoon cinnamon

Generously spray an 8 x 10-inch pan with nonstick cooking spray. Cut biscuits into fourths and arrange in pan so as much of the biscuit touches the bottom or side as possible. Generously spray biscuits with cooking spray. Combine cinnamon and sugar until blended and sprinkle over biscuits. Generously spray once more with cooking spray. Bake according to package directions. Makes 12 servings.

Nutrition information: calories 131, calories from fat 15, total fat 2 grams, saturated fat <1 gram, cholesterol 0 milligrams, sodium 478 milligrams, carbohydrate 26 grams, fiber <1 gram, sugar 9 grams, protein 3 grams. Exchanges: starch 2.

Black Forest Dessert

Prep: 8 min plus chill time

1 large package (19.8 ounces) brownie mix
¼ cup water
¼ cup baby food prune puree
½ cup egg substitute
1 large container (16 ounces) light whipped topping
16 ounce package frozen berry medley, thawed
4 tablespoons walnuts, chopped

Prepare brownie mix using water, prune puree, and egg substitute. Bake according to package directions.

Break half of brownies into bite-size pieces and arrange in a medium glass bowl. Top with half of the whipped topping, half berries, and half nuts. Be careful to spoon on each layer and spread evenly before adding the next. Repeat layers. Serve immediately. Makes 21 servings. (⅓ cup each)

Nutrition information: calories 183, calories from fat 54, total fat 6 grams, saturated fat 3 grams, cholesterol 0 milligrams, sodium 82 milligrams, carbohydrate 29 grams, fiber 1 gram, sugar 18 grams, protein 2 grams. Exchanges: starch 2, fat 1.

Variations: Use frozen raspberries or strawberries.

Note: Prune puree intensifies the chocolate flavor and keeps the brownies moist. Pureed prunes are sold in ¼ cups portions in the baby section of the grocery store.

Strawberry Dream Pie

Prep: 10 min plus chill time

1 container (8 ounces) light strawberry cream cheese, softened
1 box (1.34 ounces) sugar free cheesecake pudding
2 tablespoons skim milk
8 ounces frozen strawberry flavored whipped topping, thawed
2 cups sliced strawberries, divided
1 low fat graham cracker crust

Beat cream cheese, pudding, and milk until mixed. Fold in whipped topping. Stir in 1 cup of strawberries. Pour into pie crust. Chill for 4 hours or until set. Top with remaining strawberries just before serving. Makes 8 servings.

Nutrition information: calories 241, calories from fat 64, total fat 11 grams, saturated fat 6 grams, cholesterol 5 milligrams, sodium 267 milligrams, carbohydrate 27 grams, fiber <1 gram, sugar 11 grams, protein 4 grams. Exchanges: starch 2, fat 2.

White Chocolate Raspberry Pie

Prep: 8 min plus chill time

1 package (8 ounces) fat free cream cheese, softened
1 cup skim milk
1 teaspoon sugar free raspberry gelatin mix
1 package (3.75 ounce) instant white chocolate pudding mix
1 container (8 ounces) sugar free whipped topping
1 (6 ounce) reduced fat graham cracker crust
6 tablespoons low sugar raspberry preserves

Beat together cream cheese and milk. Add gelatin and pudding mix. Continue beating until smooth. Fold in whipped topping. Pour mixture into pie crust and refrigerate 4 hours or until firm. Serve with a tablespoon of raspberry preserves atop. Makes 6 servings.

Nutrition information: calories 275, calories from fat 64, total fat 7 grams, saturated fat 4 grams, cholesterol 8 milligrams, sodium 305 milligrams, carbohydrate 32 grams, fiber <1 gram, sugar 18 grams, protein 5 grams. Exchanges: other carbohydrate 2, very lean meat 1, milk 1/2.

Garnish with whipped topping or chocolate shavings if desired.

Citrus Fruit Dip

Prep: 6 min

1 container (6 ounces) light vanilla yogurt
1 package (8 ounces) fat free cream cheese, softened
1 tablespoon brown sugar
3 tablespoons orange juice

Mix all ingredients together until smooth. Store covered in refrigerator. Makes 32 (1 tablespoon) servings.

Nutrition information: calories 21, calories from fat 12, total fat 1 gram, saturated fat 1 gram, sodium 52 milligrams, carbohydrate 1 gram, fiber 0 grams, sugar 1 gram, protein 1 gram. Exchanges: 0.

Peanut Butter Fruit Dip

Prep: 3 min

1/4 cup low fat peanut butter
1 container (6 ounces) light vanilla yogurt
1 container (8 ounces) frozen sugar free whipped topping, thawed

Whisk together peanut butter and yogurt. Fold in whipped topping. Makes 12 (1/4 cup) servings.

Nutrition information: calories 80, calories from fat 38, total fat 4 grams, saturated fat 2 grams, cholesterol <1 milligram, sodium 37 milligrams, carbohydrate 8 grams, fiber <1 gram, sugar 3 grams, protein <1 gram. Exchanges: carbohydrate 1/2, fat 1.

Cream Cheese Fruit Dip

Prep: 3 min

1 package (8 ounces) fat free cream cheese
1 container (6 ounces) light yogurt, any variety
1 container (8 ounces) frozen sugar free whipped topping, thawed

Using a mixer, beat cream cheese and yogurt until smooth. Fold in whipped topping. Makes 12 (1/4 cup) servings.

Nutrition information: calories 60, calories from fat 22, total fat 2 grams, saturated fat 1 gram, cholesterol 3 milligrams, sodium 86 milligrams, carbohydrate 6 grams, fiber 0 grams, sugar 3 grams, protein 2 grams. Exchanges: carbohydrate 1/2.

Pumpkin Chocolate Chip Cookies

Prep: 3 min   Cook: 13-17 min

1 carrot cake mix (18.25 ounce)
1 can (15 ounces) pumpkin
1 teaspoon almond extract
2/3 cup milk chocolate chips

Preheat oven to 350 degrees.

Mix together cake mix, pumpkin, and extract. Stir in chocolate chips. Drop by spoonfuls onto a baking sheet prepared with cooking spray. Bake 13–17 minutes. Makes 24 cookies

Nutrition information: calories 129, calories from fat 34, total fat 3 grams, saturated fat 1 gram, cholesterol 0 milligrams, sodium 128 milligrams, carbohydrate 23 grams, fiber <1 gram, sugar 15 grams, protein <1 gram. Exchanges: starch 1 1/2.

Chocolate Mint Cookies

Prep: 5 min   Cook: 10 min

1 chocolate cake mix (18.25 ounce)
2 egg whites
4 tablespoons baby food prune puree
5–7 tablespoons water
15 Andes mints

Preheat oven to 350 degrees.

Mix cake mix, egg white, prune puree, and water until well blended. Drop on a cookie sheet prepared with cooking spray by the tablespoon. Bake for 10–12 minutes. Remove from oven and flatten cookie with spatula. Break mints in half. Place a piece of mint on top each warm cookie. Spread melted mint over cookie with back of spoon. Allow cookies to cool. Makes 30 servings.

Nutrition information: calories 93, calories from fat 26, fat 3 grams, saturated fat <1 gram, cholesterol 15 milligrams, sodium 80 milligrams, carbohydrate 15 grams, fiber <1 gram, sugar 9 grams, protein 1 gram. Exchanges: carbohydrate 1, fat 1/2.

Hardy Wheat Oatmeal Cookies

Prep: 12 min Bake: 10 min

1 cup packed brown sugar
½ cup butter, softened
6 egg whites or 3 egg substitute equivalents
¾ cup applesauce
2 teaspoons vanilla
2 cups quick-cooking oats
2 cups whole wheat flour
½ teaspoon cinnamon
2 tablespoons flax seed
1 teaspoon baking soda
1 teaspoon baking powder
½ teaspoon salt
1 ¼ cups semisweet mini chocolate chips
½ cup diced almonds

Preheat oven to 350 degrees.

Cream brown sugar and butter together in a mixing bowl. Beat in each egg, one at a time. Stir in applesauce and vanilla. In a separate bowl, combine all dry ingredients. Mix until well combined. Gradually combine flour mixture into creamed mixture. Stir in chocolate chips and almonds. Drop by tablespoonfuls onto a large ungreased baking sheet. Bake for 10–12 minutes until lightly golden. Makes 36 cookies.

Nutrition information: calories 88, calories from fat 34, total fat 4 grams, saturated fat 4 grams, cholesterol 5 milligrams, sodium 39 milligrams, carbohydrate 12 grams, fiber 1 gram, sugar 7 grams, protein 2 grams. Exchanges: starch 1, fat 1.

No Bake Wonders

Prep: 7 min   Cook: 1 min

3/4 cup sugar
1/2 cup skim milk
1/4 cup light margarine
3 tablespoons cocoa
1/4 teaspoon salt
1 teaspoon vanilla
1/3 cup reduced-fat creamy peanut butter
3 cups quick cooking oats

In a medium saucepan over medium heat, combine sugar, milk, margarine, and cocoa. Boil for 1 minute. Remove from heat. Immediately stir in remaining ingredients in the order listed. Drop by the tablespoonful onto a baking sheet lined with wax paper. Cool completely. Store covered in the refrigerator. Makes 36 cookies.

Nutrition information: calories 109, calories from fat 15, total fat 1 gram, saturated fat <1 gram, cholesterol <1 milligram, sodium 37 milligrams, carbohydrate 22 grams, fiber <1 gram, sugar 16 grams, protein 1 gram. Exchanges: carbohydrate 1 1/2.

The Good Stuff

Prep: 15 min plus 4 hours chill time

9 whole graham crackers
3 tablespoons butter, melted
2 small packages (1 ounce each) sugar free raspberry gelatin
2 cups boiling water
1 package (10 ounces) frozen raspberries
2 tablespoons lemon juice
1 package (8 ounces) fat free cream cheese, softened
1 tablespoon skim milk
1 container (8 ounces) frozen light whipped topping, thawed
2 tablespoons powdered sugar

Crush graham crackers to make crumbs. Combine butter with crumbs and press 3/4 of mixture into a 7 x 11-inch baking dish. Set aside. In a bowl, combine gelatin with boiling water and stir until dissolved. Add raspberries and lemon juice. Place in refrigerator for 30 minutes until partly set. In a separate bowl, beat cream cheese with milk. Stir whipped topping and powdered sugar into cream cheese mixture. Place half cream cheese mixture carefully over crust. Spoon gelatin over top cream cheese mixture. Lightly spread remaining cream cheese mixture over gelatin layer. Sprinkle remaining crumbs over the top. Chill for 3 hours. Makes 12 servings.

Nutrition information: calories 134, calories from fat 45, total fat 4 grams, saturated fat 2 grams, cholesterol 3 milligrams, sodium 182 milligrams, carbohydrate 17 grams, fiber <1 gram, sugar 7 grams, protein 3 grams. Exchanges: starch 1, fat 1.

Crust-less Pumpkin Pie Pudding

Prep: 8 min

1 cup pumpkin puree
1/2 teaspoon pumpkin pie spice
1 package (1 ounce) instant sugar-free cheesecake pudding mix
1 cup evaporated skim milk
1/2 cup skim milk

In a 2-quart bowl, combine pumpkin puree and pumpkin pie spice. Beat pudding mix and milks into the pumpkin mixture. Beat for 2 minutes until pudding starts to thicken. Refrigerate until ready to serve. Makes 6 servings.

Nutritional information: calories 70, calories from fat 2, total fat <1 gram, saturated fat <1 gram, cholesterol 2 milligrams, sodium 353 milligrams, carbohydrate 13 grams, fiber 1 gram, sugar 7 grams, protein 4 grams. Exchanges: skim milk 1.

Variation: Use an instant sugar-free butterscotch pudding or vanilla mix in place of the cheesecake pudding mix.

Peach Cobbler

Prep: 6 min   Bake: 35 min

1 can (30 ounces) reduced sugar peaches
1 (18.25 ounce) reduced sugar yellow cake mix
½ teaspoon cinnamon

Preheat oven to 350 degrees. Prepare a 9 x 13-inch baking pan with nonstick cooking spray.

Drain peaches, reserving juice. Place peaches in pan, cutting into smaller pieces if desired. Evenly sprinkle cake mix over top. Pour peach juice over cake mix. Sprinkle cinnamon over all. Cover and bake for 35–40 minutes or until slightly browned. Makes 18 (1/3 cup) servings.

Nutrition information: calories 139, total fat 1 gram, saturated fat <1 gram, cholesterol 0 milligrams, sodium 177 milligrams, carbohydrate 30 grams, fiber <1 gram, sugar 19 grams, protein 1 gram. Exchanges: starch 1 1/2, fruit 1/2.

Note: Serve with whipped topping on top.

Tips for diabetic cooking

1. When a recipe calls for oil, use heart healthy types such as olive, canola, and peanut.
2. Two egg whites can be substituted for a whole egg and contains less fat.
3. When using canned fruit, use light syrup or rinse with water to reduce carbohydrates and calories.
4. Using a reduced fat item such as cream cheese, cottage cheese, or salad dressing will give a healthier result with the same great taste.
5. Fresh or frozen vegetables have less sodium than canned and are sometimes just as inexpensive.
6. Drain ground beef in a colander under hot running tap water or pat dry with a paper towel to rid of unwanted saturated fat.
7. To prevent food poisoning, place all left over food containing eggs, meat or dairy products promptly in the refrigerator.
8. Eating a consistent amount of carbohydrates at mealtime and regular exercise can help control blood sugar.
9. Eat a large variety of fruits and vegetables to help ensure adequate vitamins in your diet. Brightly colored ones are best.
10. Skim or 1 % fat milk is healthier when compared to 2% or whole. All "white" milk is equal in vitamins, protein, and carbohydrate. It is the fat content that is different.
11. Try cooking meat in water, broth, or pan spray instead of frying in oil.
12. Check the food label. Sometimes a "sugar free" food has just as much or more carbohydrate than the regular.
13. Count carbohydrates as accurately as possible. The payoff is better blood sugar.
14. Measure foods periodically as a "reminder" of what a portion size looks like.

15. Use food labels when possible to count carbohydrates. If a label isn't available then use estimations found in carbohydrate counting books.
16. Increase the fiber and water in your diet to prevent constipation.
17. Drinking 8-10 glasses of water per day will help a person stay hydrated.
18. If you are trying to lose weight, add more steamed non-starchy vegetables to your meals. Be careful with butter and sauces.
19. Exercise will help control blood sugar, weight, cholesterol, and blood pressure.
20. At a restaurant, share the meal or take half of it you in a "doggie" bag.

Index

A

B

C

D

Steak and Rice Dinner 53
Steak, Rubbed and Salsa 52
Stew, Quick Homemade 25
Stir-Fry, Ramen Noodle 59
Stir-fry, Shrimp 101
Stir-Fry, Vegetable 45
Strawberry Delight Smoothie 13
Stuffed mushrooms 14

T

Tacos, Soft, Pork 93
Tacos, Spicy Chicken and Bean 70
Tilapia, Romano Crusted 100
Turkey, Seasoned 84
Turnovers, Apple Pie 110

V

Veggie Bites 10
Veggie Subs 47